Corporate Identity 3

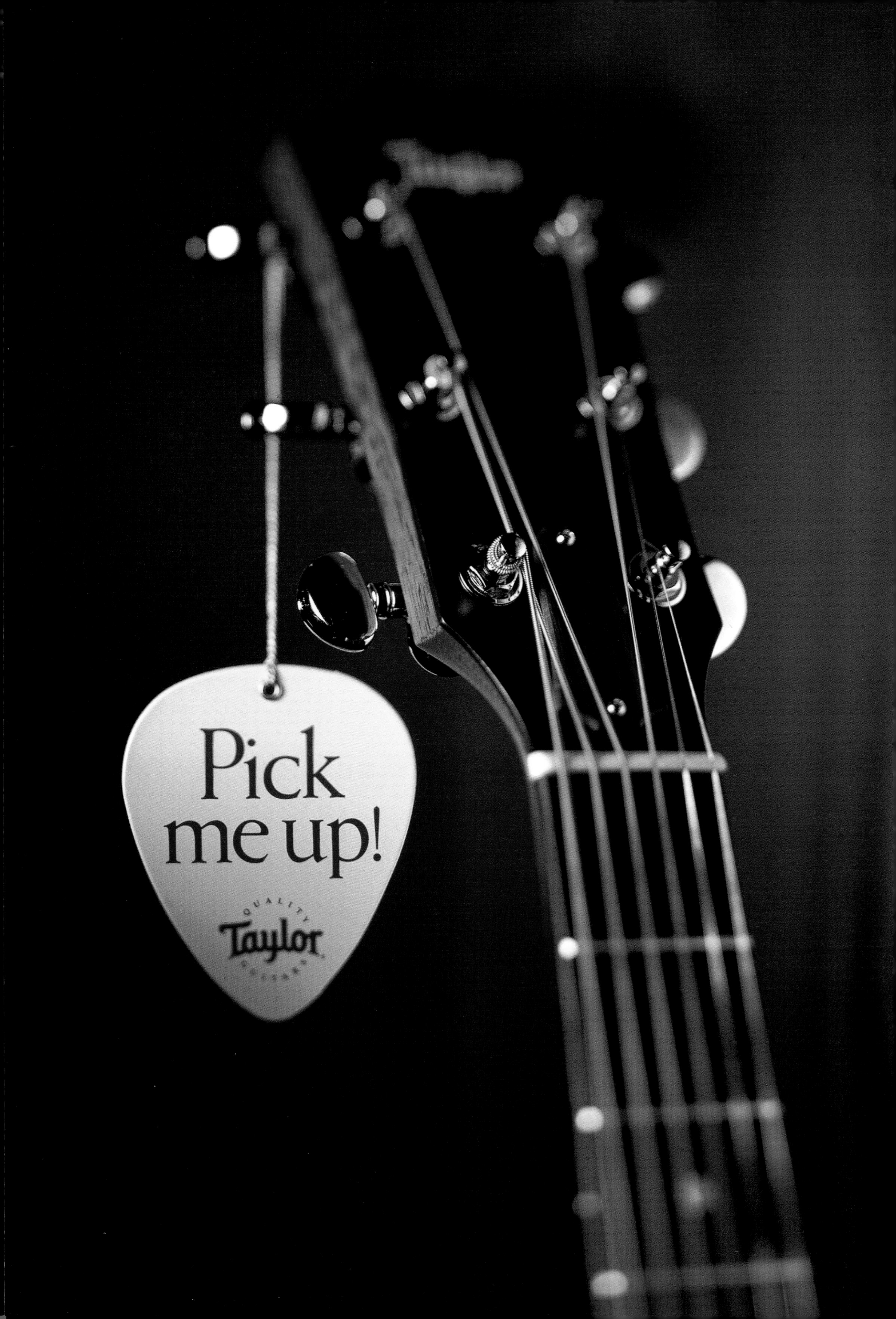
Pick
me up!
QUALITY
Taylor
GUITARS

Corporate Identity 3

An International Compilation of Corporate Identity Programs
Eine internationale Auswahl von Identitätskonzepten
Panorama international des concepts d'identité institutionnelle

Publisher and Creative Director: B. Martin Pedersen

Editors: Clare Hayden, Heinke Jenssen
Associate Editors: April Heck, Allison Xantha Miller

Art Director: Massimo Acanfora
Graphic Designers: Mei Yee Yap, Jennifer Ruf

Published by Graphis Inc.

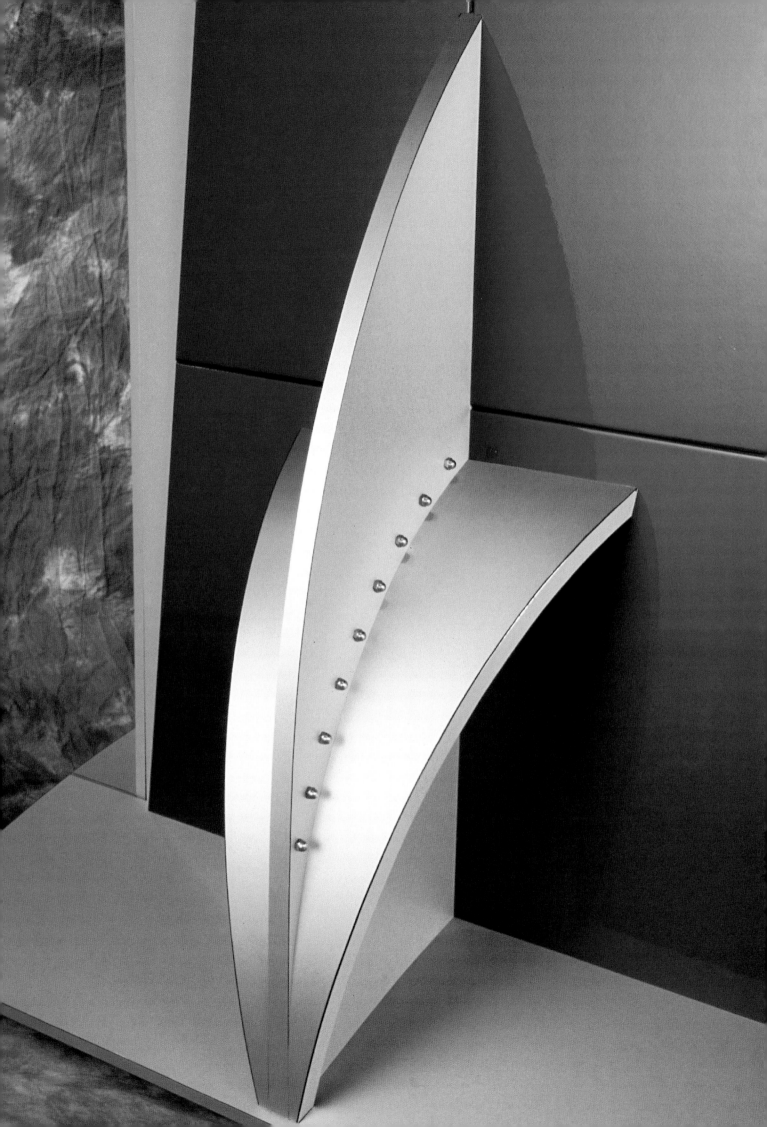

Contents Inhalt Sommaire

Remarks: We extend our heartfelt thanks to contributors throughout the world who have made it possible to publish a wide and international spectrum of the best work in this field. Entry instructions for all Graphis Books may be requested from: **Graphis Inc.**, 141 Lexington Avenue, New York, NY 10016-8193 or visit our Web site: www.graphis.com

Anmerkungen: Unser dank gilt den einsendern aus aller welt, die es unser möglicht haben, ein breites, internationales specktrum der besten arbeiten zu veröffentlichen. Teilnahmebedin-gungen für die Graphis-Bücher sind erhältlich beim: **Graphis Inc.**, 141 Lexington Avenue, NewYork, NY 10016-8193. Besuchen sie uns im World Wide Web: www.graphis.com

Remerciements: Nous remercions les participants du monde entier qui ont rendu possible la publication de cet ouvrage offrant un panorama complet des meilleurs travaux. Les modalités d'inscription peuvent être obtenues auprès de: **Graphis Inc.**, 141 Lexington Avenue, New York, NY 10016-8193. Rendez-nous vis-ites sur notre site web: www.graphis.com

(opposite) Gee + Chung Design for IBM Corp. *(following page)* Bauers Büro for Creative Modervertriebs GmbH.

On Corporate Identity: Massimo Vignelli

In Latin, "corpus" means body. From the beginning of history, men belonging to the same trade wanted to incorporate to become a recognizable body. So they formed corporations to represent and promote their trade and to protect themselves. From the Middle Ages through the Renaissance and thereafter, guilds and corporations of arts and crafts have produced delightful buildings and works of art to express the dignity and culture of their corporations. As trade organizations and private enterprises have increased in number, their means of expressing and identifying themselves to the

public have been constantly increasing in number as well as in complexity. ■ The articulation of an identity, the way it is expressed through all aspects of a corporation, becomes its image. Image is not designed; it is the public's perception of an identity or of corporate communications. Good or bad, planned or accidental, every corporation has an image. Therefore, it might as well be a good one. To be effective, a corporate identity should be the expression of an attitude of integrity, not a promotion manipulating the public. Integrity for a company means a balanced and honest relationship of all the parts involved in the production process. However, an identity may sometimes be only skin deep, just cosmetic make-up to improve appearances. This type of approach doesn't usually last very long because it eventually reveals the real nature of the company: anything phony will show its true face. The truth behind an identity program which is based on an attitude of integrity, and not on sheer promotion, will become obvious. ■ In the formulation of a corporate identity program, there are three distinct phases: semantic, syntactic, and pragmatic. The first phase, semantic, involves investigating the roots of the company—its meaning, makeup, markets, and communication history. This research is then evaluated and a strategic plan outlined to encompass the company's identity in its product, communication, and marketing aspects. The nature and depth of the first phase can vary considerably according to the size of the company and its potential. ■ The second phase, syntactic, involves the creation of a basic grammar and syntax to articulate a language that most effectively expresses the company's nature and intentions that emerged from phase one. In this phase, design concepts are elaborated in order to define the basic visual grammar that will create the visual language of the company. Indeed, the syntactical phase verifies the appropriateness of this language at all levels. In this phase, boundaries are established, including what can be done and what should not be done, how to use the existing structures, how to behave within the rules, and how to stretch them if necessary. Here the identity program begins to take shape, and the overall concept begins to take form. ■ The following phase, the pragmatic one, is the implementation of the identity program. All of the elements established in the preceding phases are considered here and organized to support the communication efforts of the company. Within this phase, attention to detail becomes extremely important, because proper implementation structures have to be set up and maintained for an identity program to succeed. The easiest structure, naturally, is for the original consultants to implement the program, as with the Knoll identity program, which was carried out entirely by our office without any formal guidelines. (As the saying goes, perhaps no one

knows how to play the music better than its composer.) However, this is not always feasible due to such factors as distance, cost, or changes in management. These and other factors can place the program at the risk of total collapse: a hundred days to build, one day to destroy. ■ As a result, it becomes more and more important to find alternatives, especially when the company wants to implement the program in-house for practical and economic reasons. Therefore, we often train the client's designers who will be implementing the program by supervising their projects in our own office for a period of time. This strategy proved most effective with Ducati, for instance, by offering us the advantage of verifying or modifying the program in the interest of obtaining the best results. ■ Another alternative is to set up an in-house design office for the client by hiring the right people ourselves. For the Benetton identity program, we created and staffed an in-house office with fifteen people to implement the program, enabling the designers to relate both to us and to the company. This kind of structure is obviously appropriate for a large company, like Benetton, which could keep such an office properly staffed and busy full time. ■ Another strategy is to consult the client's office by becoming a virtual part of their staff or by making them a virtual part of ours. For the National Park Service, we acted as direct consultants to their excellent in-house design office. Computers, ISDN, video conferencing, and modems are making all of this easier. The virtual office of the future, where one could assemble the best talents by simply connecting with them electronically, is just around the corner. It is possible that the best design offices will someday access and provide all of the necessary services not under one physical roof, but rather under one virtual global roof, where the interaction of disciplines and visualization could appear in real time, designed and fine-tuned for immediate implementation. Indeed, for Cosmit, the organizing committee of the Salone de Mobile, Milan, we designed a graphic program in Milan and New York, working via ISDN. ■ Of all the phases involved in creating a successful corporate identity program, the implementation is the most delicate to bring to fruition because it is the most vulnerable to mediocre talents. Just as it is possible today to achieve the best typography ever in the history of printing, it is also true that the same capacities make the worst-ever available—it all depends on the intelligence and talent of the designer. It is my hope that the technological developments we are experiencing will provide the opportunity for the best talents to achieve the best work, and for them to lead the pack. The office of tomorrow could provide the most exceptional corporate identity programs ever. The chance is just next door.

*Born in Milan, **Massimo Vignelli** was the co-founder of Unimark International Corporation in 1965, and later opened the offices of Vignelli Associates (1971) and Vignelli Design (1978). His work includes graphic and corporate identity programs, architectural graphics, and exhibition, interior, and consumer-product designs for leading international companies. Museums such as the Museum of Modern Art, the Metropolitan Museum of Art, and the Brooklyn Museum have entered his work in their permanent collections. A past president of AGI and AIGA, Vignelli has received many awards, including the first Presidential Design Award, the National Arts Club Gold Medal, the Interior Product Designers Fellowship of Excellence, and The Brooklyn Museum Design Award for Lifetime Achievement.*

(opposite) Portrait of Massimo Vignelli by Luca Vignelli

Erscheinungsbild: Massimo Vignelli

Seit Menschengedenken war Angehörigen derselben Zunft daran gelegen, als eine Einheit, eine erkennbare Körperschaft aufzutreten. Deshalb gründeten sie Körperschaften, welche die Interessen ihrer Zunft wahrnehmen und ihre Mitglieder schützen sollten. Im Mittelalter, in der Renaissance und auch danach haben die Kunst– und Handwerkszünfte eindrucksvolle Gebäude und Kunstwerke geschaffen, um die Würde und Kultur ihrer Körperschaften zum Ausdruck zu bringen. Mit der wachsenden Zahl von Organisationen und privaten Unternehmen

wurden die Strategien zur Selbstdarstellung in der Öffentlichkeit immer komplexer. ■ Die Formulierung der Identität, die Art, wie sie in allen Unternehmensbereichen zum Ausdruck kommt, wird zum Image. Ein Image kann man nicht gestalten; es entsteht in den Köpfen des Publikums aufgrund einer Identität oder der Kommunikation einer Firma. Gut oder schlecht, geplant oder zufällig – jedes Unternehmen hat ein Image, warum also kein gutes. Um wirksam zu sein, sollte das Erscheinungsbild einer Firma Ausdruck einer integren Haltung sein und nicht eine durch Werbung erreichte Manipulierung des Publikums. Integrität bedeutet bei Unternehmen ein ausgewogenes und aufrichtiges Verhältnis zu allen, die am Herstellungsprozess beteiligt sind. Ein Erscheinungsbild ist unter Umständen jedoch nur aufgetragen, Kosmetik, um die Firma besser aussehen zu lassen. Das ist jedoch meistens nicht von langer Dauer, weil die wahre Natur der Firma irgendwann durchscheint: Jeder Schwindel fliegt einmal auf. Andererseits wird sich ein Erscheinungsbild, das auf einer integren Haltung beruht und nicht nur auf oberflächlicher Werbung, als wahr erweisen. ■ Bei der Formulierung eines C.I.-Programms gibt es drei klare Phasen: die semantische, die syntaktische und die pragmatische. ■ In der ersten, der semantischen Phase, geht es darum, mehr über die Ursprünge des Unternehmens herauszufinden, über Bedeutung, Aufbau, Märkte und das Wesen seiner Kommunikation. Diese Untersuchungen werden dann ausgewertet, und es wird eine Strategie entwickelt, um alle Aspekte der Firmenidentität in ihre Erzeugnisse, in die Kommunikation und ins Marketing einfliessen zu lassen. Art und Umfang der ersten Phase variiert erheblich je nach Grösse und Potential der betroffenen Firma. ■ Zur zweiten, der syntaktischen Phase gehört die Schaffung einer grundsätzlichen Grammatik und Syntax, um eine Sprache zu entwickeln, die die Art und Intentionen der Firma, die sich aus der ersten Phase ergeben haben, auf bestmögliche Weise zum Ausdruck bringt. In dieser Phase werden die Design-Konzepte erarbeitet, um die grundlegende visuelle Grammatik festzulegen, welche die visuelle Sprache der Firma prägen wird. In der syntaktischen Phase wird die Eignung dieser Sprache auf allen Ebenen überprüft. Und in dieser Phase werden die Grenzen gesetzt, auch dafür, was machbar ist und was nicht getan werden sollte, es wird festgelegt, wie die erstellten Strukturen benutzt werden sollen, wie man sich im Rahmen der Regeln verhält und wie man sie, wenn nötig, ausbaut. An diesem Punkt nehmen Konzept und C.I-Programm allmählich Form an. ■ Dann folgt die pragmatische Phase, die Umsetzung des C.I.-Programms. Alle

in den vorangegangenen Phasen festgelegten Elemente werden jetzt formuliert und geordnet. In dieser Phase wird die Beachtung von Details äusserst wichtig, weil Strukturen für die Umsetzung geschaffen und eingehalten werden müssen, wenn das Programm Erfolg haben soll. Am einfachsten ist es natürlich, wenn die Designer, die das C.I.-Programm entwickelt haben, es auch später umsetzen. Unser Büro hat z.B. das visuelle Erscheinungsbild für Knoll vollständig umgesetzt, und zwar ohne formelle Richtlinien. (Vielleicht spielt niemand die Musik besser als der Komponist.) Das ist jedoch aus verschiedenen Gründen nicht immer möglich, sei es wegen der Distanz oder Kosten oder aufgrund eines Wechsels in der Geschäftsleitung. Diese und andere Faktoren können ein Programm vollkommen zunichte machen: Hundert Tage für den Aufbau, ein Tag für die Zerstörung. ■ Deshalb wird es immer wichtiger, Alternativen zu finden, besonders wenn der Kunde aus praktischen und wirtschaftlichen Gründen das Programm selbst umsetzen möchte. Wir instruieren dann die Gestalter, die dafür zuständig sein werden, indem wir sie für eine gewisse Zeit in unserem Atelier unter unserer Aufsicht an den Projekten arbeiten lassen. Dieses Vorgehen erwies sich bei unserem Kunden Ducati als sehr erfolgreich. Wir können dadurch das Programm prüfen und eventuell noch abändern, um die bestmöglichen Resultate zu erzielen. ■ Eine andere Möglichkeit ist, für den Kunden ein internes Design-Büro zu organisieren, indem wir die geeigneten Leute für ihn finden. Beim Erscheinungsbild für Benetton bauten wir das interne Büro auf und besorgten fünfzehn Mitarbeiter für die Durchsetzung des Programms. So wird eine geeignete Struktur geschaffen, und die Designer stehen mit uns und dem Auftraggeber in Verbindung; für eine grosse Firma wie Benetton, die sich ein solches Büro leisten und ständig beschäftigen kann, ist das zweifellos die richtige Lösung. ■ Eine weitere Alternative besteht darin, dass wir entweder ein virtueller Teil des betreffenden Kunden werden oder er ein virtueller Teil unserer Firma. Beim National Parks Service wurden wir zu direkten Beratern ihres hervorragenden internen Design-Studios. Computer, ISDN, Video-Konferenzen und Modem sind dabei eine grosse Erleichterung. Das virtuelle Büro der Zukunft, bei dem man die besten Leute zusammenbringen kann, indem man sie einfach elektronisch miteinander verbindet, ist nicht mehr fern. Es ist durchaus möglich, dass die besten Design-Studios der nahen Zukunft Zugang zu allen gewünschten Dienstleistungen haben und sie dem Auftaggeber zwar nicht unter einem realen Dach zur Verfügung stellen können, wohl aber unter einem virtuellen, globalen Dach, wo das Ineinandergreifen der ver-

Massimo Vignelli, gebürtiger Mailänder, war Mitbegründer der Unimark International Corporation (1965) und eröffnete 1971 eine eigene Firma, Vignelli Associates, und 1978 Vignelli Design. Das Spektrum seiner Tätigkeiten umfasst Graphik- und C.I.-Design, Architekturgraphik, Ausstellungsdesign, Innenarchitektur und Design im Konsumgüterbereich für führende internationale Unternehmen. Seine Arbeiten wurden in zahlreichen Ausstellungen und Zeitschriften in aller Welt vorgestellt. Zudem ist er in den Sammlungen verschiedener Museen vertreten, u.a. im Museum of Modern Art und im Metropolitan Museum, New York, sowie im Brooklyn Museum. Er war Präsident der AGI (Alliance Graphique Internationale) und des AIGA (American Institute of Graphic Arts). Zu den zahlreichen Auszeichnungen, die er erhalten hat, gehören aus der jüngeren Zeit der Presidential Design Award, die Goldmedaille des National Arts Club, das Interior Product Designers Fellowship of Excellence und der Brooklyn Museum Design Award for Lifetime Achievement.

schiedenen Bereiche und die Visualisierung in Realzeit statt-finden könnten, für die sofortige Anwendung entworfen und bis ins Detail abgestimmt und ausgearbeitet. Für Cosmit, die Organisatoren der Mailänder Möbelmesse, haben wir ein graphisches Programm direkt in Mailand bzw. in New York ent-worfen, wobei wir via ISDN arbeiteten. ■ Von all den Phasen der Erarbeitung eines erfolgreichen visuellen Erschei-nungsbildes ist die Umsetzung die delikateste, weil mittelmässig begabte Designer leicht alles kaputtmachen können. Es ist wie mit der Typographie – mit den heutigen Mitteln ist es möglich,

die beste typographische Gestaltung in der Geschichte des Drucks zu machen, aber auch die schlechteste. Alles hängt von der Intelligenz und vom Talent des Benutzers ab. Ich hoffe, dass die technologischen Entwicklungen unserer Zeit dazu führen werden, dass die Begabtesten eingesetzt werden können, um die bestmöglichen Resultate zu erzielen, und dass sie für die anderen Vorbild sein werden. Das Büro von morgen sollte in der Lage sein, die intelligentesten und raffiniertesten visuellen Erscheinungsbilder aller Zeiten zu entwickeln. Wir sind nicht weit davon entfernt.

Vignelli Associates designed the graphic indentity for Cosmit, (the organizing committee of the Salone de Mobile, Milano) by working with the client in Italy via ISDN.

Vignelli Associates entwickelten das graphische C.I.-Programm für Cosmit (Organisationskomitee des Salone di Mobile in Mailand) in Zusammenarbeit mit dem Kunden via ISDN.

Vignelli Associates a créé le programme d'identité graphique de Cosmit (le comité organisateur du Salone de Mobile, Milan) en travaillant avec le client via le RNIS.

Design: Massimo Vignelli/ Dani Piderman

Milano

To replace the brochures, folders and posters that Cosmit used previously, Vignelli Associates designed an A4-size folder. When this is first opened, it becomes an A3-size page; opened again it becomes an A2-size poster, so that the pace at which the information is conveyed interacts with the folding and vice versa. The folder was an economical way to increase impact and exposure.

Anstelle der bisher von Cosmit verwendeten Broschüren, Mappen und Plakate entwarfen Vignelli Associates eine Faltmappe im A4-Format. Wenn man sie öffnet, erhält man eine Seite im A3-Format, die ihrerseits nach nochmaligem Auseinanderfalten zu einem A2-Plakat wird. Auf diese Weise wird die Information Stuck für Stück sichtbar. Die Faltmappe war eine kostenguunstige, effiziente und äusserst werbewirksame Lösung.

Pour remplacer les brochures, porte-documents et affiches utilisées par Cosmit, l'agence Vignelli Associates a conçu une chemise pliable de format A4. En l'ouvrant, on découvre une feuille de format A3 qui, une fois dépliée, présente une affiche de format A2. De cette façon, l'information est délivrée pièce par pièce. Une solution bon marché et efficace qui a eu un grand impact publicitaire.

Design: Massimo Vignelli/
Dani Piderman

Milan est une ville dont la forte vivacité naît du culte de la profession que l'on y exerce, de sa capacité de favoriser l'activité des individus, de la quantité de ressources économiques qui s'y concentrent. Les opérateurs de la mode et de la communication, le monde de l'industrie et celui du tertiaire avancé, les personnes qui travaillent à la Scala et celles qui s'occupent de design: des professions brillantes qui se sont affrontées ici très sérieusement. Ne pensez-vous pas que tous ces gens, à la personnalité si exigente, puissent trouver d'autres raisons que le travail, pour vivre dans cette ville ? Peut-être certains sont-ils de véritables amateurs de bonne cuisine ou des amants de l'architecture, passionnés d'art antique ou contemporain. Ou s'agit-il seulement d'amants de la vie nocturne? A Milan, c'est là le dilemme.

Identité institutionnelle: Massimo Vignelli

En Latin, "corpus" signifie corps. Depuis la nuit des temps, les hommes exerçant un même métier ont désiré se regrouper au sein d'associations pour former un corps distinct. Aussi fondèrent-ils des corporations en vue de représenter leur activité, de la promouvoir et de défendre leurs intérêts. Du Moyen Age à la Renaissance et par la suite, les guildes et les corporations des arts et métiers ont réalisé des constructions et des œuvres d'art superbes dans le but d'exprimer la dignité et la culture inhérentes à leur corporation. Pourtant, au fur et à mesure que les organisations professionelles

et les entreprises privées se multiplient, les stratégies qu'elles utilisent pour s'exprimer et s'identifier auprès du public gagnent en complexité. ■ L'articulation de l'identité, la manière dont elle est traduite à travers tous les aspects d'une association, devient l'image de la corporation. L'image n'est pas un design, c'est la perception qu'a le public d'une identité ou d'un type spécifique de communication d'entreprise. Bonne ou mauvaise, pla-nifiée ou aléatoire, chaque corporation a une image. Pour être efficace, une identité institutionnelle devrait être l'expression d'une attitude intègre et non pas d'une manipulation promotionnelle du public. L'intégrité pour une compagnie signifie que les relations entre toutes les parties impliquées dans le processus de production sont équilibrées et honnêtes. Or, une identité peut aussi se résumer à un camouflage, à une simple opération cosmétique. En général, ce type d'approche ne fait pas long feu dans la mesure où la vraie nature d'une société se révèle toujours un jour ou l'autre: tout ce qui est factice révèle son vrai visage. Mais lorsqu'un programme d'identité repose sur une attitude intègre et non pas sur une opération promotionnelle calculée, la vérité finit par triompher. ■ La formulation d'un programme d'identité institutionnelle s'articule autour de trois phases distinctes: la sémantique, la syntaxe et le pragmatisme. La première phase, la sémantique, vise à acquérir de plus amples connaissances sur les racines de la compagnie, sa signification, ses éléments constitutifs, ses marchés et sur l'histoire de sa communication. Une fois évalués, les résultats de cette recherche servent à tracer les grandes lignes d'un plan stratégique qui englobera tous les aspects de l'identité de la société, tant au niveau de ses produits, de sa communication que de ses efforts de marketing. La nature et l'ampleur de cette première phase varient considérablement en fonction de la taille et du potentiel d'une société. ■ La deuxième phase, la syntaxe, porte sur la création d'une grammaire et d'une syntaxe de base dans le but de trouver le langage le plus approprié à la nature et aux intentions de la société cristallisées autour de la première phase. Lors de cette phase, les concepts de design sont élaborés pour définir la grammaire visuelle de base à appliquer et déboucher ainsi sur le langage visuel d'une société. De fait, la phase syntaxique va consister à vérifier l'adéquation du langage à tous les niveaux. C'est à ce moment que l'on va fixer des limites, décider de ce qui peut être fait ou ne doit pas être fait,

déterminer la manière dont les structures établies seront utilisées, comment évoluer à l'intérieur de ces règles et, si nécessaire, comment les étendre. A ce niveau, le programme d'identité et le concept commencent à prendre forme. ■ La phase suivante, le pragmatisme, vise à mettre en œuvre le programme d'identité. Tous les éléments définis au cours des phases précédentes sont utilisés ici pour organiser l'information comme support de la communication. Durant cette phase, le soin apporté aux détails devient crucial, les véritables structures d'exécution devant être mises sur pied et maintenues pour garantir le succès du programme d'identité. La solution la plus facile pour mettre en place le programme serait, évidemment, de recourir aux consultants de la première heure, comme ce fut le cas pour le programme d'identité de Knoll que notre bureau a entièrement exécuté sans devoir se plier à aucune directive formelle. (Peut-être que personne ne joue mieux une partition que le compositeur lui-même.) Néanmoins, cette manière de procéder n'est pas toujours possible pour des raisons de distance, de coûts ou de changements au sein du management. Ces facteurs, parmi tant d'autres, risquent d'anéantir le programme: cent jours pour construire, un jour pour détruire! ■ Aussi est-il primordial de trouver d'autres solutions, notamment lorsqu'une société désire exécuter son programme sur place pour des considérations pratiques et économiques. Voilà pourquoi nous invitons souvent les designers du client chargés d'exécuter le programme à venir travailler un certain temps chez nous. Ainsi, nous pouvons les instruire et superviser directement leurs réalisations. Cette stratégie s'est avérée très efficace pour Ducati. Elle nous offre l'avantage de pouvoir contrôler ou modifier le programme en vue d'obtenir les meilleurs résultats. ■ Une autre possibilité consiste à mettre sur pied un bureau de designers interne pour le client en engageant nous-mêmes les bonnes personnes. Dans le cadre de l'exécution du programme d'identité de Benetton, nous avons créé une cellule de travail interne constituée de 15 colla- borateurs sélectionnés par nos soins. Cette solution permet d'établir une structure propre dans laquelle les designers peuvent s'en référer à nous et à la société. Elle est tout à fait appropriée dans le cas d'une importante société comme Benetton, car celle-ci a les moyens d'occuper à plein temps des designers. ■ Une autre option vise à consulter le bureau du client en devenant un élément virtuel de son équipe ou en faisant de

*Cofondateur d'Unimark International Corporation en 1965, le Milanais **Massimo Vignelli** a ouvert sa propre société Vignelli Associates en 1971 et son agence Vignelli Design en 1978. Le spectre de ses activités comprend le design graphique, des programmes d'identité institutionnelle, le graphisme architectural, des concepts d'exposition, l'architecture d'intérieur et le design de produits de consommation pour des entreprises leader sur le marché international. Moult articles et expositions ont été consacrés à ses travaux. En outre, ses productions figurent dans des musées prestigieux, tels que le Museum of Modern Art, le Metropolitan Museum à New York et le Brooklyn Museum. Massimo Vignelli a occupé le poste de président de l'Alliance Graphique Internationale (AGI) et de l'American Institute of Graphic Arts (AIGA). Parmi les nombreux prix qui lui ont été décernés figurent, entre autres, le Presidential Design Award, la médaille d'or du National Arts Club, l'Interior Product Designers Fellowship of Excellence et le Brooklyn Museum Design Award for Lifetime Achievement.*

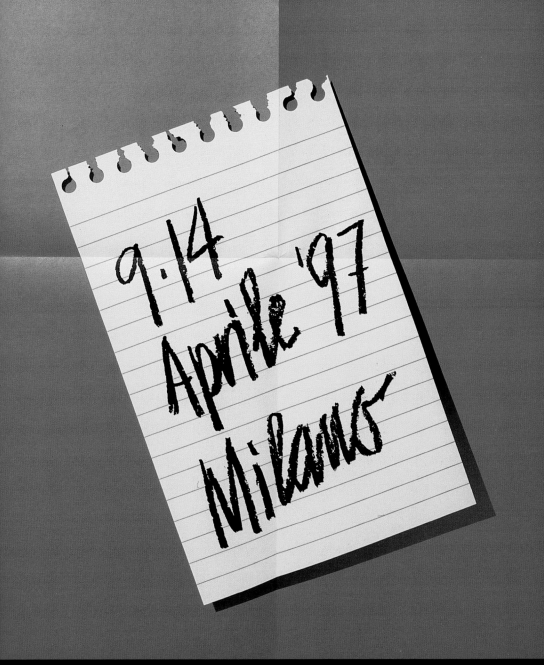

Salone Internazionale del Mobile
in concomitanza con
Eurocucina–Salone dei Mobili per Cucina
Salone del Complemento d'Arredo

9·14
Aprile '97
Milano

The central spread of a folder/poster
announcing the opening of the
Salone del Mobile.

Auseinandergefaltete Seite aus
einer Mappe, die zum Plakat wird
und die Eröffnung des Salone
del Mobile ankündigt.

Affiche dépliée extraite d'une
chemise annonçant l'ouverture
du Salone del Mobile.

Design: Massimo Vignelli/
Dani Piderman

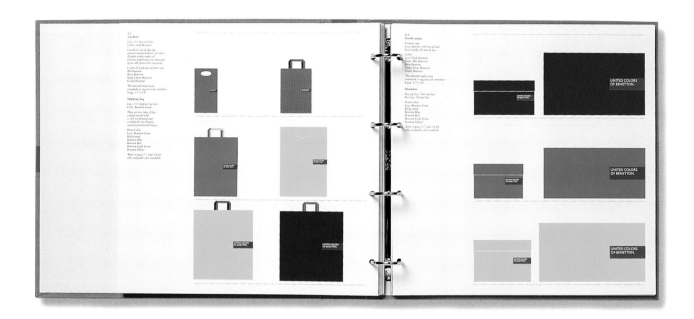

Manuale di Identificazione Coordinata
Corporate Identity Manual

UNITED COLORS
OF BENETTON.

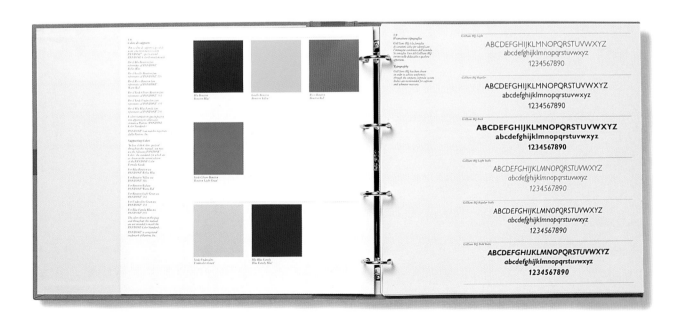

son équipe un élément virtuel de la nôtre. Pour le National Parks Service, nous étions les consultants directs de leur excellent bureau de des- igners. Les ordinateurs, le RNIS (réseau numérique à intégration de services), les vidéoconférences et les modems facilitent bien sûr ce genre d'entreprise. Le bureau virtuel du futur, où les plus grands talents seront connectés via l'électronique, se profile à l'horizon. Il est possible que, dans un proche avenir, les meilleures agences de design accéderont à tous les services nécessaires et les offriront aux clients non pas en travaillant sous un toit physique, mais sous un toit virtuel global où l'interaction des disciplines et la visualisation se feront en temps réel avec, à l'appui, des designs peaufinés dans les moindres détails et prêts à être réalisés. Pour Cosmit, le comité organisateur du Salone del Mobile à Milan, nous avons créé le programme graphique directement à Milan et à New York

en travaillant via le RNIS. ■ Parmi toutes les phases relatives à un programme d'identité institutionnelle, celle de l'exécution est la plus délicate, car elle ne résiste pas à la médiocrité des talents. Aujourd'hui, il est vrai que les moyens dont nous disposons nous permettent de créer la meilleure typographie jamais réalisée dans l'histoire de l'imprimerie, mais il est tout aussi vrai que ces mêmes moyens nous permettent de créer ce qu'il y a de pire. Tout dépend de l'intelligence et du talent de l'utilisateur. J'espère que les développements technologiques en cours nous permettront de recourir aux plus grands talents pour arriver aux meilleurs résultats possibles et que ceux-ci montreront la voie à suivre. Le bureau de demain pourrait produire les programmes d'identité institutionnelle les plus intelligents et les plus accomplis jamais réalisés. Cette opportunité est à portée de main.

(this spread)
United Colors of Benetton
Corporate Identity Manual.
The existing logo was redesigned
to become the matrix of the entire
graphic program.

United Colors of Benetton
Corporate Identity Manual.
Das Logo wurde überarbeitet
und wurde zur Basis des gesamten
graphischen Programmes.

United Colors of Benetton
Manuel d'identité institutionnelle.
Une fois retravaille, le logo a
constitué la base tout le programme
graphique.

Design: Massimo Vignelli
Text and production:
Cristina Castaldello

United Colors of Benetton
Catalogs for the Children Collections.

(this page)
This catalog is made like a deck of
cards, enabling buyers to collect cards
reflecting their choices; these cards
would eventually become the catalog
for their area of sales.

(opposite page)
This catalog offers similar opportunity.
Eventually every sales area could
receive a customized catalog reflecting
buyers' selections. The catalogs are A6 size.

United Colors of Benetton
Kataloge für die Kinder-Kollection.

(diese Seite)
Der Katalog wurde wie ein Karten-
spiel konzipiert: Die Einkaüfer
Franchise-Läden können die Karten
entsprechend den von ihnen gewünschten
Kleindungsstücken auswählen und mit-
nehmen. Sie erhalten so einen eigenen
Katalog für ihren Veraufsdistrikt.

(gegenüber)
Diese Katalog ist ähnlich konzipiert.
Aufgrund ihrer Auswahl erhieten
schliesslich alle Franchise-Läden einen
Katalog (im Format A6).

United Colors of Benetton
Catalogue de la collection enfants.

(ci–contre)
Le catalogue s'inspire d'un jeu de
cartes: les dépositaires de la marque
choisissent et empotentles cartes qui
représentent les vêtements qu'ils
aimeraient vendre. Ainsi, ils peuvent
constituer leur propre catalogue pour
leur point de vente.

(ci–contre)
Ce catalogue repose sur le même
concept. Chaque district de ventes a
obtenu un catalogue personnalisé
reflétant le choix de vêtements
effectué par les revendeurs.

Design: Massimo Vignelli/
Piera Brunetta/Naama Amitai

Fitness Fusion™ MX

Un nuovo modello per performance ad alto livello.
Telaio e inclinazione del gambetto regolabili, adatto a ruote
con diametro fino a 80mm. Freno ABT™
e leve microregolabili.

Ruote: Kryptonics® Turbo Core™ 78mm/78A. **Cuscinetti:** Killer Bees™ ABEC 5.
Lubrificazione a grasso. **Freno:** ABT™ (Active Brake Technology™).
Scarpetta interna: Traspirabilità eccezionale. **Telaio:** Monopezzo in nylon rinforzato.
Rigido, per massime sollecitazioni. **Scafo:** Struttura a sovrapposizione. **Chiusura:** 3
leve microregolabili. **Misure:** 23.0 - 32.0

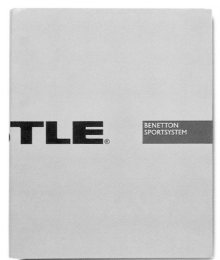

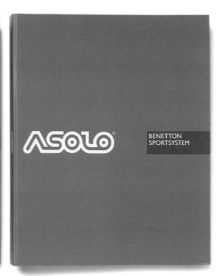

(opposite page)
Brochures for Asolo and Rollerblade.

(this page, top)
Benetton SportSystem. Binders for
the brands Kästle, Nordica and Asolo
using existing logos.

(this page, bottom)
Folder for Nordica boots.

(gegenüber)
Broschüren für Asolo und Rollerblade.

(diese Seite oben)
Benetton SportSystem.Mappen für
die Marken Kästle, Nordica und
Asolo, wobei die vorhandenen Logos
verwendet wurden.

(diese Seite unten)
Mappe für Nordica-Stiefel

(ci-contre)
Brochures pour Asolo et Rollerblade.

(page d'en-haut)
Benetton SportSystem. Chemise pourvues
des logos Kästle, Nordica et Asolo.

(page du bas)
Chemise pour les chaussures de
ski Nordica.

Design: Massimo Vignelli/
Francesca Sartorato
Photography: Attilio Vianello

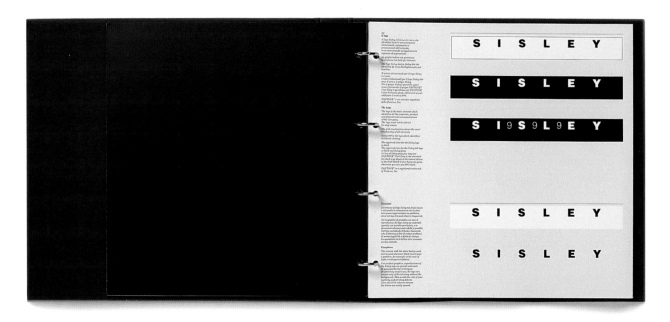

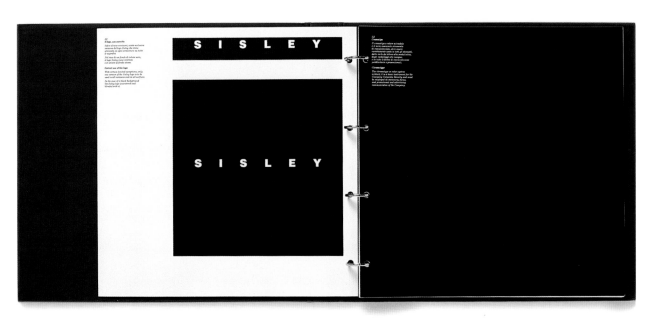

(this page)
Sisley Collection Catalog. The photography in the entire book contains a black background to emphasize the new chromotype.

(diese Seite)
Kollektionskatalog von Sisley. Alle Aufnahmen im Katalog haben einen schwarzen Hintergrund, um den neuen Farbdruck hevorzuheben.

(cette page)
Catalogue de la collection Sisley. Toute les prises de vues du catalogue ont été réalisées sur fond noir pour faire ressortir l'impression couleur.

Design: Massimo Vignelli/ Gaia Marano/ Stefano Malobbia

(opposite page)
Sisley Corporate Identity Manual of graphic standards.

(gegenüber)
Sisley Corporate Identity Manual für die graphische Gestaltung.

(ci-contre)
Manuel d'identité institutionnelle de Sisley consacré aux concepts graphiques.

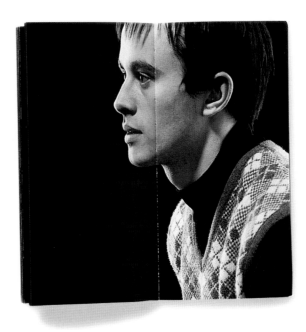

Catch the Spirit! by Richelle J. Huff

I woke up this morning and turned on CNN to catch the news. I brushed my teeth with Colgate. Cleaned my face with Ivory soap. Washed my hair with Head 'n' Shoulders. Dried myself with Ralph Lauren towels. Put on my Calvin Klein underwear. Zipped up my Gap jeans. And threw on my Eddie Bauer sweater. I was late for work so I jumped in my Jeep Cherokee and hit the McDonald's drive-thru for an Egg McMuffin. I passed on their coffee in favor of a Starbucks café latté to go. On the way to work I passed a Toys R Us and made a mental note to stop on the

way home to get a Tickle Me Elmo for my son Walker—along with some Huggies at the K-mart. ■ We live in an era when brand names have become the nation's—if not the world's—second language. It's a language built on the colorful foundation of our consumer-product history: Band-Aid, created by a Johnson & Johnson employee whose wife kept burning her fingers on the kitchen stove; Gerber, born in Michigan after Dan Gerber's own baby was switched to solid foods; Dr. Pepper, an eager young pharmacist's soda fountain experiment named for his sweetheart's disapproving father; and Ivory soap, a divine inspiration received by Harley Procter (of Procter & Gamble fame) while half-listening to a minister's Sunday sermon and trying to come up with a name for his new white soap: "out of the ivory palaces, whereby they have made thee glad." The nation's favorite soap was named for Psalms 45:8.

From spiritual to Spirit Branding™ But for all the power of a brand name, we may still be left with an empty feeling if companies don't exude that other something special I call Spirit Branding. It's that intangible sense of who the company is, not just what it sells. It's what makes the difference between being a brand we've grown up with and being one we've grown to love. And it's done especially well by companies that target kids. Take Gap. Gap knows itself. Even though adults buy Gap products, they'll never be Gap Kids—who exude a certain spirit, live a certain lifestyle. ■ Branding was once thought to be the stuff of smoke and mirrors and traveling snake-oil salesmen. Paul Rand gave the definition of branding some dignity, saying it conveyed what is unique and memorable about a company. That's still true today, but now companies must also reflect the spirit that produces the unique and memorable, and project a certain honesty while doing so. It's blowing away the smoke and shattering the mirrors to let us see clearly and exactly how in tune a company is with the environment. How its operations are helping—or hurting—the world. It is, as they say, walking the talk. And it may be why a certain well-known athletic-shoe company highly targeted towards kids is receiving negative press for allegedly using child labor to produce its products.

The fine (fuzzy) line between branding and Spirit Branding Beyond differentiating a company or its products from the competition, Spirit Branding somehow reassures consumers who are increasingly savvy and suspicious of marketing ploys. Branding controls identity and consistently communicates the image an organization wants to have. Spirit Branding, on the other hand, is what brings this identity—especially that of a many-tentacled conglomerate—down to earth, to the level of the people, to those who

buy its products. If you think of establishing—and maintaining—a corporate identity on a continuum from developing a signature or adding a signature mark, to giving that mark meaning and adding a positioning phrase that talks to key audiences, Spirit Branding is just the next step in the process. ■ Smart companies, like Coca-Cola, have done Spirit Branding from the start. Who can forget "I'd like to teach the world to sing" and the rainbow of faces on the mountaintop? Amazingly, Coke's basic identity hasn't changed much over the years. Its packaging has been updated, but its corporate identity, image, and brand have become so intertwined that the identity is the brand, and vice versa. Likewise, this working together of identity, image, and brand has led to the transformation of many trademarked names into regular nouns and even verbs: I need a Kleenex, for example, and please Xerox that page. ■ Coke's secret to marketing the spirit of its company has been to let its brand and identity share the job. Zip, Iomega, Java, Continental, and Gillette are other good examples. But the best example of Spirit Branding is the upbeat new commercial for Intel's Pentium computer chip, where a group of groovin' space-suit-clad engineers are so obviously enjoying their jobs that you want to pick up the phone and find out how to join them. The spirit of the company is driving this message, with identity and brand wrapped around it to create a nice little package that isn't really a product at all. That is, you can't buy it off the shelf; it's intangible, it's a feeling, it's the spirit of the company. And in this case, it's worth millions.

Know thyself. And thine customer To make Spirit Branding a reality, a company must know itself and its market. That could mean (shudder) doing research. Take First Team Sports and its Ultra Wheels in-line skates. In a quite competitive industry, First Team Sports knew it needed to cast off its dated, sluggish image to survive. It talked to its target market: an enthusiastic, 19- to 35-year-old, middle- to upper-income group that enjoyed life sports, especially skating. It even invited some of this group to sit on the project team for the logo redesign. The end result was an appropriately high-powered and peppy new identity that conveyed the energy of the sport and the spirit of its consumers. ■ While First Team Sports shows how a newer company leveraged the powers of Spirit Branding, the Gillette Company is an example of how an older company's foray into Spirit Branding breathed new life into its many products and companies. For years, the Gillette Company's name was perceived to be about men's shaving razors and blades. In reality, the Gillette Company owns Paper Mate, Braun, Oral B, and Waterman. But the company needed a face-lift to convey the diversity of its consumer brand franchises while recognizing the

*Originally from Fargo, North Dakota, **Richelle Huff** spent 16 years in New York before heading to Minnesota with the hope that global warming will soon make it a more temperate place to live. Huff is a vice president at Larsen Design + Interactive, a Minneapolis-based design firm, where she consults with Fortune 500 companies such as Boston Scientific, Fairview Health Services, and Northern States Power (NSP) on their spirit branding and marketing systems. Formerly of Lippincott & Marquilies in New York, she consulted on branding and identity programs for Continental Airlines, the Gillette Company, IBM, ITT Hartford , and the St. Paul Companies. Prior to that, she was art director at Progressive Architecture magazine. She was also an associate art director at CBS's Cuisine magazine and a former designer at M+Co. with Tibor Kalmon. She received her M.F.A. from Cranbrook Academy of Art.*

equity of its past. Today, a redesigned logo differentiates the company's corporate image from its brand image. A new identity statement, "World-Class Brands, Products, People," clarifies the company's total breadth and depth and adds value to all the brands operating under the Gillette Company umbrella. ■ The use of brands, logos, and visual communication to promote products or services has been around as long as people have had things to sell. And visual communication is powerful: initial impressions are lasting ones (ask any couple who fell in love at first sight!), proven by the fact that approximately 85 percent of the information we glean from life comes from just one of our senses— sight. Unfortunately, the art of design has not always been valued

compete not only with each other, but with lack of understanding and confusion on the part of the consumer. Novellus Systems, a semiconductor-chip manufacturer, wanted to produce a high-tech and entertaining exhibit for the industry's largest trade show. It also wanted to educate visitors about the angstrom, a small unit of measurement used in Novellus data storage systems. That challenge could have caused at least a little angst (!) for the design firm, but with a thorough understanding of the company and its spirit, the designers created the intriguing "Angstromania" exhibit theme, along with an engaging interactive exhibit and collateral materials, all of which ultimately helped quadruple exhibit attendance. ■ The bottom line is that because there are so many

as a way to create that lasting impression. But it should be. **How to capture the spirit** Spirit Branding depends on the ability of designers to understand the company's overall strategy, products, and services, and transform that knowledge into that intangible thing or magic about the company that makes it different from its competitors. It's not just putting a logo on a piece of paper. It's the total image of the company and what it does, including its marketing messages, business strategy, and the way that the company and its products make you feel. With Spirit Branding, designers are capturing the essence of a company, not just creating a poster, package or brochure. ■ This can be harder to do in high-tech industries where complex, obscure products

brands to choose from in almost any category, companies have to find ways to make their brands work harder. Spirit Branding can help do this. ■ Remember this as you are sitting in your Herman Miller chair, reading the *Wall Street Journal*, sipping a Coke, one ear toward your Mitsubishi big-screen TV, while your Lean Cuisine cooks in the Sharp microwave....

(opposite)
First Team Sports - Ultrawheels packaging.
Design firm: Larsen Design+Interactive.
Photographed by Ripsaw Photography, Minneapolis, MN.

(above)
Novellus - Angstromania 2 Materials.
Design firm: Larsen Design+Interactive.
Photographed by Ripsaw Photography, Minneapolis, MN.

Das gewisse Etwas von Richelle J. Huff

Ich wachte heute morgen auf und stellte CNN an, um die Nachrichten zu hören. Ich putzte die Zähne mit Colgate; wusch mein Gesicht mit Ivory-Seife und mein Haar mit Head 'n' Shoulders. Zum Abtrocknen nahm ich Handtücher von Ralph Lauren, zog meine Calvin-Klein-Unterwäsche an, dann die Gap-Jeans und meinen Eddie-Bauer-Pullover. Ich war ein bisschen spät dran, also stieg ich in meinen Cherokee-Jeep und fuhr zu McDonald's, wo ich mir vom Auto aus einen Egg McMuffin besorgte. Ihren Kaffee verschmähte ich zugungsten eines Milchkaffees von Starbuck. Auf dem Weg zur Arbeit kam ich an einem Toys R Us vorbei und nahm mir vor, am Abend ein

Tamagotchi für meinen Sohn Walker zu holen. ■ Wir leben in einer Zeit, in der Markennamen zur Sprache eines Landes – wenn nicht der Welt – geworden sind. Es ist eine Sprache, die sich aus der farbigen Geschichte der Konsumprodukte entwickelt hat: Band-Aid (vergleichbar mit Hansaplast), wurde von einem Angestellten der Firma Johnson & Johnson erdacht, dessen Frau sich ständig die Finger am Herd verbrannte; Gerber-Babynahrung erblickte in Michigan das Licht der Welt, nachdem Dan Gerbers eigenes Baby an feste Nahrung gewöhnt wurde; Dr. Pepper's geht auf die Idee eines ehrgeizigen jungen Apothekers zu einem Ausschank alkoholfreier Getränke zurück, den er nach dem Vater seiner Liebsten nannte (der übrigens nicht mit ihm einverstanden war); und Ivory-Seife ist eine Eingebung, die Harley Procter (von Procter & Gamble) bei der Sonntagspredigt hatte, als seine Gedanken um einen Namen für eine neue weisse Seife kreisten «...wenn du aus den elfenbeinernen Palästen daher-trittst in deiner schönen Pracht». Die Lieblingsseife der Nation («Elfenbein»-Seife) erhielt ihren Namen dank Psalm 45:9.

Vom innerlichen zum 'Spirit Branding' Wie stark auch ein Markenname sein mag, man verspürt eine gewisse Leere, wenn Firmen nicht noch zusätzlich etwas ausstrahlen, das ich 'Spirit Branding' nenne. Es ist dieses nicht greifbare Gefühl dessen, was eine Firma darstellt, unabhängig von den Produkten, die sie verkauft. Das macht auch den Unterschied aus zwischen einer Marke, mit der wir aufgewachsen sind, und einer Marke, die wir schätzen gelernt haben. Firmen, deren Zielpublikum Kinder sind, sind Meister im Spirit Branding. Der Textilhersteller Gap zum Beispiel beherrscht die Gap-«Kultur» bis in die Fingerspitzen. Obgleich auch Erwachsene Gap-Produkte kaufen, werden sie nie Gap-Kinder sein, die ein gewisses Etwas, eine gewisse Lebensart ausstrahlen. ■ Branding war früher etwas, das mit dem Rauch von Brandeisen für die Kennzeichnung der Rinder und mit obskuren Markenartikeln umherreisender Quacksalber in Verbindung gebracht wurde, bis Paul Rand dem Begriff Würde verlieh, indem er ihn als das definierte, was an einer Firma ein-

*Die ursprünglich aus Fargo, Nord-Dakota, stammende **Richelle Huff** lebte 16 Jahre in New York, bevor sie nach Minnesota zurückkehrte, in der Hoffnung, dass die globale Erwärmung die Temperaturen dieser Gegend angenehmer machen würde. Huff ist Vize-Präsidentin von Larsen Design + Interactive, eine Design-Firma mit Sitz in Minneapolis, wo sie Firmen, die auf der Fortune-500-Liste zu finden sind – Boston Scientific, Fairview Health Services und Northern*

States Power (NSP)–, hinsichtlich ihres 'Spirit Branding' und der Marketing-Programme berät. Als sie noch für Lippincott & Marquilies in New York tätig war, beriet sie Continental Airlines, Gillette Company, IBM, ITT Hartford und die St. Paul Companies im Hinblick auf die Branding- und C.I.-Programme. Sie war ausserdem Associate Art Director bei der von CBS her-ausgegebenen Zeit-schrift Cuisine und hat als Graphikerin mit Tibor Kalman für M+Co.

malig und bemerkenswert ist. Das hat noch immer Gültigkeit, aber heute müssen Firmen auch den Geist, der das Einzigartige und Bemerkenswerte schafft, zum Ausdruck bringen und dabei glaubwürdig wirken. Der Rauch wurde weggeblasen, um klar zu erkennen, wie das Verhältnis der Firma zur Umwelt ist, inwieweit ihre Operationen der Welt helfen oder sie schädigen. Eine Firma wird auf Herz und Nieren geprüft. Zurzeit hat zum Beispiel ein sehr bekannter Hersteller von Sportschuhen, dessen Zielpublikum vor allem junge Leute sind, sehr viel schlechte Presse, weil er angeblich Kinderarbeit in seiner Schuhproduktion benutzt.

Die feine Linie zwischen Branding und Spirit Branding
Abgesehen davon, dass Spirit Branding eine Firma oder ihre Produkte von der Konkurrenz unterscheiden hilft, stellt Spirit Branding auch beim immer wachsameren und kritischeren Konsumenten ein gewisses Vertrauen her. Branding prägt das Erscheinungsbild und vermittelt das von der Firma gewünschte Image konsequent. Image Branding andererseits ist das, was dieses Erscheinungsbild – besonders das von vielarmigen Konglomeraten – auf den Boden der Realität bringt, auf die Ebene der Leute, derjenigen, die die Produkte der Firma kaufen. Wenn Sie daran denken, ein Erscheinungsbild aufzubauen und zu erhalten, in einem fortlaufenden Prozess, ausgehend von der Entwicklung eines Schriftzugs oder eines Markenzeichens, diesem eine Bedeutung geben und mit einigen Worten ausdrücken wollen, die das Zielpublikum ansprechen, so ist Spirit Branding der nächste Schritt in diesem Prozess. ■ Schlaue Firmen wie Coca Cola haben von Anfang an Spirit Branding betrieben. Jeder Amerikaner kennt das 'I'd like to teach the world to sing' und den Regenbogen von Gesichtern über den Berggipfeln. Erstaunlicherweise hat sich Coca Colas Erscheinungsbild über die Jahre kaum verändert. Die Verpackung wurde ein bisschen aufgefrischt, aber die Corporate Identity, das Image und die Marke sind so eng miteinander verwoben, dass das Erscheinungsbild die Marke ist und umgekehrt. So hat dieses Zusammenspiel von Erscheinungsbild, Image und Marke dazu geführt, dass Markennamen an die Stelle von regulären Substantiven oder gar Verben getreten sind, wie zum Beispiel 'Hast du ein Kleenex für mich?' oder 'Bitte Xerox (photokopiere) diese Seite'. ■ Coca Colas Geheimnis beim Vermarkten des Geistes der Firma war, Marke und Firmen-Image gleichermassen zu nutzen. Es gibt noch mehr gute Beispiele, das beste ist allerdings der neue TV-Spot für Intels Pentium-Prozessor, in dem eine Gruppe von Technikern, die in chicen Raumanzügen stecken, mit so viel offensichtlicher Begeisterung bei der Arbeit sind, dass man zum Telephon greifen möchte, um herauszufinden, ob man nicht mit ihnen arbeiten könnte. Der Geist der Firma trägt diese Botschaft, die kombiniert mit Image und Marke ein nettes kleines Paket abgibt, das eigentlich kein Produkt ist. Das heisst, es ist etwas nicht Greifbares, es ist ein Gefühl, es ist der Geist der Firma. In diesem Fall ist es Millionen wert.

Erkenne dich selbst und deinen Kunden Um Spirit Branding in die Tat umzusetzen, muss eine Firma sich und ihren Markt kennen. Das könnte bedeuten, dass man Marktforschung machen muss. Man denke an First Team Sports und seine Inline-Skates mit dem Markennamen Ultra Wheels. Hier gibt es ziemlich viel Konkurrenz, und die Firma First Team Sports wusste, dass sie, um zu überleben, ihr reichlich verstaubtes und etwas lahmes Image loswerden musste. Die Firma sprach mit ihrer Zielgruppe: begeisterungsfähige junge Leute zwischen 19 und 35 Jahren mit mittleren bis hohen Einkommen, die gerne Sport treiben, besonders Inline-Skating. Einige von ihnen wurden sogar eingeladen, sich mit dem Projekt-Team zusammenzusetzen.

das mit der Auffrischung des Logos betraut war. Das Endergebnis war ein entsprechend rasantes neues Erscheinungsbild mit viel Pep, das dem Geist der Sportart und ihrer Anhänger entsprach. ■ Während First Team Sports zeigt, wie eine jüngere Firma 'Spirit Branding' zu ihrem Vorteil nutzen kann, ist die Firma Gillette ein Beispiel dafür, wie eine ältere Firma durch Spirit Branding ihren zahlreichen Produkten und Unternehmen ein neues Gesicht gab. Jahrelang verstand man unter Gillette allgemein eine Firma, die Rasiermesser und Klingen für Männer herstellt. Tatsächlich aber besitzt Gillette Paper Mate, Braun, Oral B und Waterman. Die Firma brauchte unbedingt ein Facelifting, um die Vielfalt ihrer Produkte zum Ausdruck zu bringen, ohne auf den Bonus des soliden alten Rufes zu verzichten. Ein überarbeitetes Logo unterscheidet das Firmen-Image heute vom Marken-Image. Stichworte im Zusammenhang mit dem neuen Erscheinungsbild – «Weltklassemarken, Produkte, Menschen» – verdeutlichen den gesamten Unternehmensbereich der Firma und werten alle Marken unter dem Gillette-Dach auf. ■ Seit die Menschen etwas zu verkaufen haben, werden Marken, Logos und visuelle Kommunikation in der Werbung für Produkte oder Dienstleistungen verwendet. Visuelle Kommunikation ist dabei von grosser Bedeutung: die ersten Eindrücke sind ausschlaggebend (fragen Sie alle, die sich auf den ersten Blick verliebt haben!) – es ist eine erwiesene Tatsache, dass wir ca. 85% der Information unserer Umgebung nur durch einen unserer Sinne aufnehmen, das Sehvermögen. Leider wurde nicht immer erkannt, dass Graphik ein Mittel ist, das diesen bleibenden Eindruck schaffen kann. Das wäre aber wünschenswert.

Wie man den Geist einfängt Spirit Branding hängt von der Fähigkeit der Designer ab, die Gesamtheit der Firmenstrategie, der Produkte und Dienstleistungen zu erfassen und diese Erkenntnis in jene nicht fassbare Sache bzw. jenen Zauber umzusetzen, der die Firma von der Konkurrenz unterscheidet. Es geht nicht nur darum, ein Logo auf ein Blatt Papier zu setzen. Es ist das gesamte Image der Firma und ihrer Aktivitäten, einschliesslich der Marketing-Botschaften, der Geschäftsstrategie und des Gefühls, das die Firma und ihre Produkte den Konsumenten geben. Beim Spirit Branding erfassen die Designer das Wesen einer Firma, sie entwerfen nicht einfach ein Plakat, eine Verpackung oder eine Broschüre. ■ Die Aufgabe ist besonders in der High-Tech-Branche schwierig, in der komplexe, schwer fassbare Produkte es nicht nur mit der Konkurrenz aufnehmen müssen, sondern auch mit Unkenntnis und Verwirrung auf Seiten der Verbraucher. Novellus Systems, Hersteller von Halbleiter-Chips, wollte einen High-Tech- und doch unterhaltsamen Stand für die grösste Fachmesse der Branche. Ausserdem sollten die Besucher über den *Angstrom* aufgeklärt werden, eine kleine Messeinheit, die im Datenspeichersystem von Novellus verwendet wird. Diese Herausforderung hätte der Designfirma durchaus *Angst* machen können, aber dank ihrer gründlichen Kenntnis der Firma und des Firmengeistes fanden die Designer ein über-zeugendes Ausstellungsthema – «Angstromania» – für eine fesselnde, interaktive Ausstellung und sämtliche Unterlagen. Das führte zu einer Besucherzahl, die viermal höher war als erwartet. ■ Weil so viele Marken zur Auswahl stehen, bedeutet das im Endeffekt, dass Firmen Wege finden müssen, damit ihre Marken mehr leisten. Spirit Branding kann dies unterstützen. ■ Denken Sie daran, wenn Sie in Ihrem Knoll-Stuhl sitzen, das *Wall Street Journal* lesen, eine Coca Cola trinken, ein Ohr auf den Mitsubishi-Fernseher

Ce petit quelque chose en plus par Richelle J. Huff

Ce matin, au saut du lit, j'ai allumé CNN pour regarder les infos. Je me suis brossé les dents avec du Pepsodent, débarbouillée à la hâte avec ma savonnette Ivory et lavé les cheveux avec du shampoing Klorane. Je me suis séchée avec des serviettes Ralph Lauren, j'ai enfilé mes dessous Calvin Klein et fermé la braguette de mes Levi's. Puis, j'ai enfilé mon chandail Benetton. Comme j'étais en retard, je me suis précipitée dans ma Jeep Cherokee et j'ai fait une halte au prochain McDonald's où j'ai avalé en vitesse un EggMcMuffin. J'ai renoncé à leur lavasse, préférant un bon petit noir de chez Starbuck's. Sur le chemin pour aller au travail, je suis passée devant un Toys R Us et je me suis dit qu'en rentrant, je ferais un crochet pour acheter un Tamagotchi à mon fils Walker.

Nous vivons à une époque où les marques sont devenues la langue de la nation, si ce n'est du monde. Une langue qui s'est développée à travers l'histoire haute en couleur des produits de consommation: le Band-Aid (notre sparadrap) a été inventé par un employé de la société Johnson & Johnson, dont la femme se brûlait régulièrement les doigts en mitonnant de bons petits plats; les petits pots Gerber ont vu le jour dans le Michigan, après que le bébé de Dan Gerber eut passé du lait à une nourriture plus consistante; Dr. Pepper est l'invention d'un jeune pharmacien ambitieux, qui désirait ouvrir un débit de boissons non alcoolisées – il le baptisa d'après le nom du père de sa dulcinée (celui-ci désapprouvait d'ailleurs tout à fait cette idée); quant au savon Ivory, on le doit à une inspiration divine de Harley Procter de Procter & Gamble qui, alors qu'il écoutait d'une oreille distraite la messe du dimanche, se demanda comment il pourrait bien appeler son nouveau savon blanc comme neige: «Dans les palais d'ivoire les instruments à cordes te réjouissent.» C'est ainsi que le psaume 45:9 donna un nom au savon fétiche de tout un pays. ■ **De l'état d'esprit au 'spirit branding'** Peu importe l'impact d'un nom de marque, on ressent un certain vide si une société n'arrive pas à transmettre ce petit quelque chose en plus que j'appelle 'spirit branding'. C'est cette impression générale, impalpable, cet état d'esprit que l'on associe à une société, indépendamment des produits qu'elle vend. Là réside la différence entre une marque avec laquelle on a grandi et une autre que l'on a appris à apprécier au fil du temps. Les sociétés dont le public cible est constitué d'enfants sont passées maître dans l'art du spirit branding. Le fabricant de vêtements Gap, par exemple, maîtrise la «culture» Gap sur le bout des doigts. Bien que les adultes achètent aussi les produits de la marque, ils ne seront jamais des enfants Gap, avec leur état d'esprit et leur style de vie bien à eux. Autrefois, on associait le mot «branding» (marquage d'une marchandise ou du bétail au fer rouge et, dans un sens plus large, choix et exploitation d'une marque) tantôt à de la fumée, dans le cas du bétail, tantôt à quelque chose de flou, voire de douteux, à l'image des colporteurs dont les intentions paraissaient toujours malhonnêtes jusqu'au jour où Paul Rand ennoblit ce terme, le définissant comme cette particularité qui rend une société unique et remarquable. Aujourd'hui, cette acception demeure valable, mais les sociétés se doivent de refléter cet état d'esprit qui les rend justement uniques, remarquables et crédibles. La fumée s'est dissipée et, entre-temps, les colporteurs ont été renvoyés chez eux. Désormais, il convient d'identifier clairement quelle est la relation d'une société avec son environnement, dans quelle mesure ses opérations sont salutaires ou nuisibles. Toute entreprise est passée au crible, et c'est là que le bât blesse. Pour preuve: ce célèbre fabricant de chaussures de sport qui récolte actuellement une si mauvaise presse parce qu'il fait travailler des enfants au rabais! ■ **La nuance subtile entre branding et spirit branding** S'il contribue à démarquer une société et ses produits de la concurrence, le spirit branding permet aussi de gagner la confiance du consommateur devenu plus critique et plus attentif et de le rassurer. Le nom de marque et son développement jouent un rôle décisif sur l'identité visuelle et véhiculent donc l'image que souhaite avoir une société. Quant au spirit branding, il jette un pont entre le consommateur et l'identité visuelle - en particulier, celle d'importants conglomérats –, amène cette dernière au sol des réalités, au niveau des consommateurs qui achètent les produits de la société. Si vous avez l'intention de façonner et de conserver une identité visuelle en commençant par trouver un nom de marque ou un logo pour le développer par la suite en lui donnant une signification qu'il s'agira d'exprimer en quelques mots susceptibles de séduire le public cible, alors le spirit branding sera la prochaine étape de ce processus continu. ■ Des sociétés intelligentes comme Coca-Cola ont fait du spirit branding dès le début. Chaque Américain se souvient de la headline «I'd like to teach the world to sing» et de la montagne coiffée d'un arc-en-ciel formé de visages. Etonnamment, l'identité visuelle de Coca-Cola n'a que très peu changé au fil des ans. Le packaging a subi un léger lifting, mais l'identité visuelle, l'image et la marque sont si intimement liées que l'identité visuelle est devenue la marque et vice versa. Cette relation étroite entre identité visuelle, image et marque explique pourquoi les noms de marque remplacent parfois des substantifs ou des verbes – «T'aurais pas un Kleenex?» ou «Je l'ai scotché sur le frigo.» ■ Pour véhiculer l'esprit de la société, Coca-Cola a misé à parts égales sur la marque et l'image de l'entreprise. De fait, les bons exemples ne manquent pas, mais le meilleur est peut-être le nouveau spot pour les processeurs Intel Pentium: un groupe d'ingénieurs, habillés en cosmonaute, est en train de travailler avec un enthousiasme tel qu'on a envie de décrocher le téléphone et de leur demander comment les rejoindre. L'esprit de la société porte le message qui, combiné à l'image et à la marque, forme un tout séduisant. Un tout qui n'est pas un produit en réalité – rien de saisissable ni de palpable donc. C'est l'état d'esprit de la société, et dans ce cas, cela vaut des millions.

■ **Connais-toi toi-même et connais tes clients!** Pour faire du spirit branding, une société doit savoir qui elle est et connaître son marché. Cela pourrait signifier qu'il faille procéder à des études de marché. Prenons l'exemple de First Team Sports et de ses in-line skates appelés Ultra Wheels. Dans un secteur où la concurrence est rude, la société First Team Sports savait que, pour survivre, elle devrait se débarrasser de son image poussiéreuse. Elle s'est donc adressée à son groupe cible composé de jeunes gens enthousiastes âgés 19 à 35 ans, bénéficiant de revenus moyens à élevés et pratiquant volontiers un sport, en particulier le in-line skating, et est allée jusqu'à inviter certains d'entre eux à collaborer au toilettage du logo en participant aux séances de l'équipe de designers chargée du projet. Le résultat: une identité visuelle radicalement nouvelle, dynamique et pétillante, à l'image de l'état d'esprit inhérent aux accros du roller en ligne. ■ Tandis que First Team Sports exemplifie comment une jeune société peut tirer avantage du spirit branding, l'entreprise Gillette montre comment une entreprise de longue tradition a su dynamiser l'image de ses nombreux produits et sociétés. Durant de longues années, on considérait Gillette comme un fabricant de lames et de rasoirs jetables. En réalité, Gillette possède les produits Paper Mate, Braun, Oral B et Waterman. Elle avait donc besoin d'un bon lifting pour représenter sa vaste gamme de produits sans renoncer pour autant à son excellente réputation. Un logo revisité distingue aujourd'hui l'identité institutionnelle de l'image de marque. Une nouvelle accroche relative à son identité – «Des marques de classe mondiale, des produits, des hommes» – témoigne de l'étendue de ses activités et rehausse en même temps la valeur de chaque marque dans la mesure où elle est assimilée à la longue tradition Gillette. ■ Depuis le jour où les hommes se sont mis à vendre des produits, les marques, les logos et la communication visuelle ont servi à promouvoir des produits et des prestations de services. Dans ce contexte, la communication visuelle joue un rôle clé: les premières impressions sont déterminantes (demandez autour de vous combien de personnes ont eu un coup de foudre!); il est prouvé que nous percevons 85% des informations de notre environnement uniquement par l'un de nos sens, la vue. Par contre, on ne reconnaît toujours pas, et c'est regrettable, que le graphisme représente un moyen efficace pour faire perdurer cette première impression. ■ **Comment capturer l'esprit** Le spirit branding dépend de la faculté du designer à saisir la stratégie d'entreprise dans son ensemble, ses produits et ses prestations de services et à les transformer, tel un magicien, en quelque chose d'impalpable, d'unique, afin de démarquer la société de ses concurrents. Il ne s'agit pas uniquement de coucher un logo sur une feuille de pa- pier. C'est un tout, l'image globale de la société, ses activités, les messages marketing, la stratégie d'entreprise et l'impression qui se dégage de la société et de ses produits auprès des consommateurs. La finalité du spirit branding consiste à capturer l'essence d'une société; la tâche des designers ne se limite pas à créer une affiche, un packaging ou une brochure. ■ Une tâche ardue, notamment dans le secteur de la technologie de pointe où des produits complexes, incompréhensibles, doivent non seulement s'affirmer face à la concurrence, mais aussi dissiper la confusion du consommateur, son manque de connaissances. A l'occasion du plus grand salon d'exposition de la branche, Novellus Systems, fabricant de puces, désirait un stand à la fois high-tech et divertissant. En outre, les visiteurs devaient être initiés à l'angstrom, une petite unité de mesure utilisée dans le système d'enregistrement de données Novellus. Un défi de cette taille aurait pu effrayer l'agence de design chargée du projet, mais grâce à ses connaissances approfondies de la société et de son esprit, les designers trouvèrent un thème d'exposition intriguant et convaincant – «Angstromania» –, associé à une exposition interactive stimulante et décliné sur tous les supports publicitaires. L'afflux de visiteurs enthousiastes dépassa de loin les attentes de la société. ■ La multitude de marques proposées sur le marché est telle que les sociétés se voient contraintes de trouver de nouveaux moyens pour rendre leurs marques plus performantes. Le spirit branding s'inscrit dans cette optique. ■ Pensez-y lorsque vous êtes assis sur votre chaise Ikea en train de lire le *Wall Street Journal* et de boire un Coca-Cola, un œil rivé sur votre téléviseur grand écran Mitsubishi tandis que votre menu minceur Findus cuit dans votre micro-ondes Seb.

*Originaire de Fargo dans le nord du Dakota, **Richelle Huff** a vécu pendant 16 ans à New York avant de retourner dans le Minnesota en espérant y trouver des températures plus clémentes. Vice-présidente de Larsen Design + Interactive, Richelle Huff travaille dans cette agence de design basée à Minneapolis en tant que conseillère de sociétés répertoriées dans Fortune 500, dont Boston Scientific, Fairview Health Services et Northern States Power (NSP). Son activité de consultante porte essentiellement sur le spirit branding et des programmes de market-*

ing. A l'époque où elle était employée chez Lippincott & Marquiries à New York, elle comptait parmi ses clients Continental Airlines, Gillette Company, IBM, ITT Hartford et St. Paul Companies et était spécialisée dans les programmes d'identité visuelle et le développement de noms de marque. En outre, elle a occupé le poste de directrice artistique adjointe au magazine Cuisine édité par CBS et a collaboré en tant que graphiste avec Tibor Kalman pour M+Co. Elle a obtenu un Master of Fine Arts de la Cranbrook Academy of Art.

Corporate Identity 3

Communication Arts Company
Craig Singleton Hollomon Architects

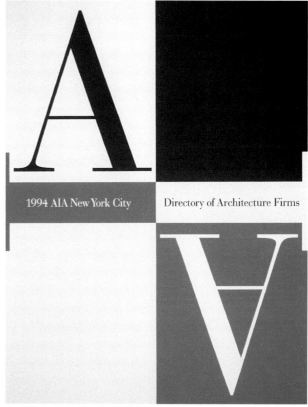

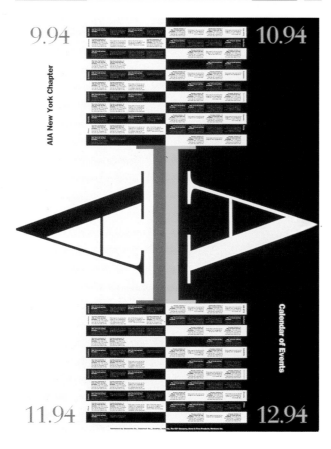

Pentagram Design
American Institute of Architects

(this spread)
George P. Johnson Co.
Nissan Corporation

(this spread)
Fitch Inc.
Chrysler Corporation

Mires Design
Hot Rod Hell

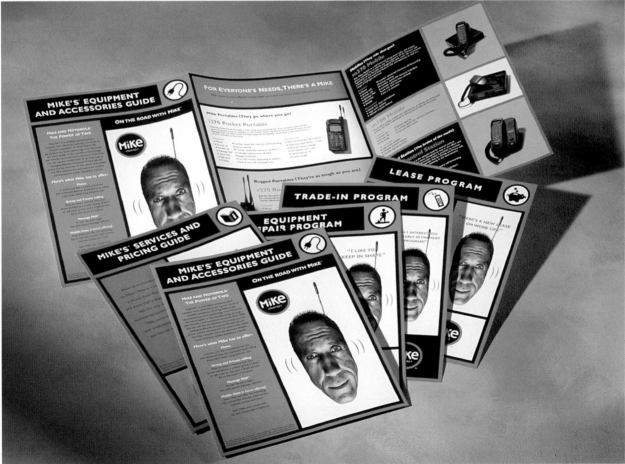

TAXI Design
Clearnet

(this spread)
Hornall Anderson Design Works
Nextlink Corporation

(this spread)
Hornall Anderson Design Works
Intermation Corporation

Title: **IBM Software Station Kiosk**

Description: **This "software vending machine" utilizes satellite transmission to enable customers to demo, place orders and take delivery of the latest software directly from the kiosk.**

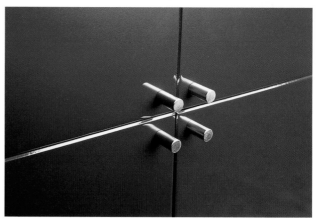

(this spread)
Gee & Chung Design
IBM Corporation

Pentagram Design
Computer Film Company

Geer Design
Times 3 Productions

FAST

NO.	CLASSIFICATION
NUMBER OF WORDS	
YEAR FILED	

TEL. 804 358 9366

WORK™

FAX 804 358 9421

DIRECT

COMMENTS
RE.	

ADVERTISING AND CONSULTING SERVICES
NO JOB IS TOO LARGE OR TOO SMALL

2019 MONUMENT AVENUE · RICHMOND · VIRGINIA · 23220 · U.S.A.

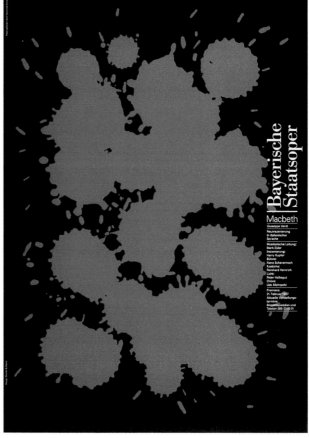

(this spread)
Mendell & Oberer
Bavarian State Opera

(this spread)
Pentagram Design
The Public Theater

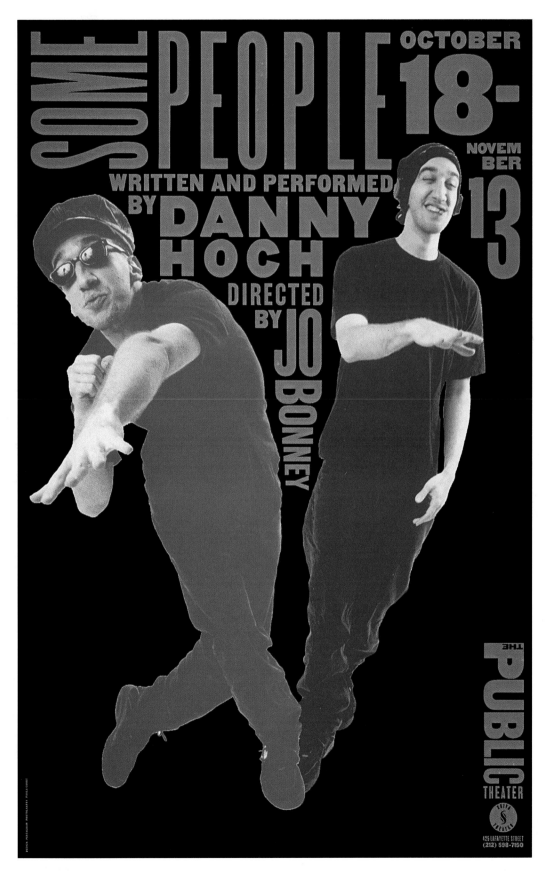

(this spread)
Pentagram Design
The Public Theater

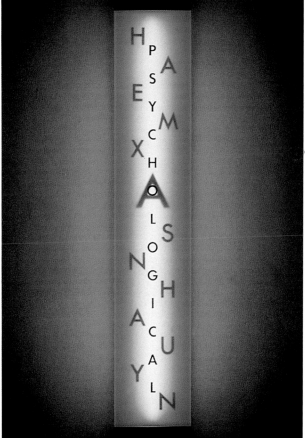

(opposite)
BJ Krivanek
California Tower

(this page)
BJ Krivanek
In-house

(previous spread, this page bottom)
BJ Krivanek
Union Rescue Mission, Los Angeles

(this page top)
BJ Krivanek
Jefferson High School, Los Angeles

(this page)
BJ Krivanek
Union Rescue Mission, Los Angeles

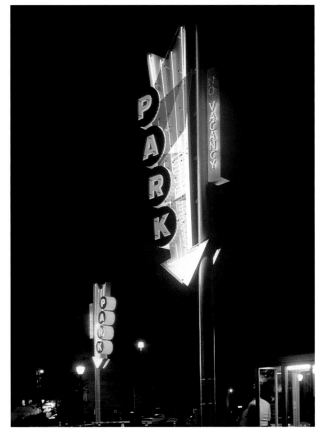

(this spread)
Kiku Obata & Co.
Grand Center

(this spread)
Pentagram Design
The Fashion Center

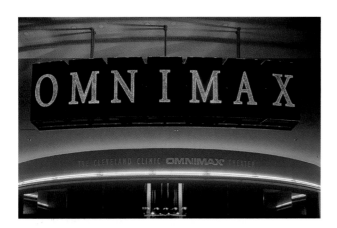

(this spread)
Kiku Obata & Co.
Great Lakes Science Center

Sussman/Prejza & Co., Inc.
City of Santa Monica, CA

Clifford Selbert Design Collaborative
Salem State College

(this spread)
Werkhaus Design
Snohomish County Parks Dept.

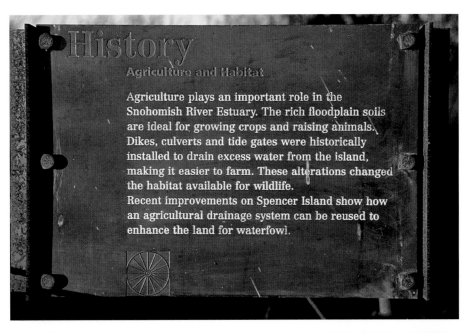

(this spread)
Nicholson Design
City of National City, CA

(this spread)
Desgrippes Gobé & Associates
Ann Taylor Inc.

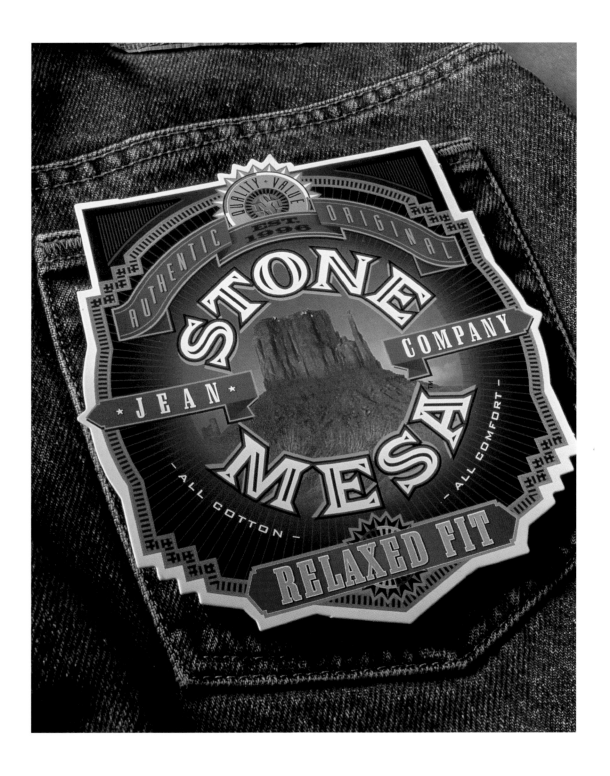

(this spread)
Phoenix Creative
Venture Design Group

(opposite top left)
Phoenix Creative
Venture Design Group

(opposite top right, bottom; this page)
Venture Design Group
Venture Stores

(this spread)
Sagmeister Inc.
Blue

THIS COLOR IS BLUE!

Look at the small black point in the center of the cross in the orange field for 20 seconds. Then look at the small black point in the grey field. The orange field will appear blue. And that's the way it's meant to be.

On Thursday 3.3.1994 we will open BLUE Clothing stores in Bregenz, Dornbirn, and Feldkirch.

(this spread)
Sagmeister Inc.
Blue

(this spread)
Zimmerman Crowe
Levi's

(this spread)
Zimmerman Crowe
Levi's

(this spread)
Mires Design
Adventure 16

(this spread)
Haley Johnson Design Co.
Goldsmith, Agio, Helms & Co.

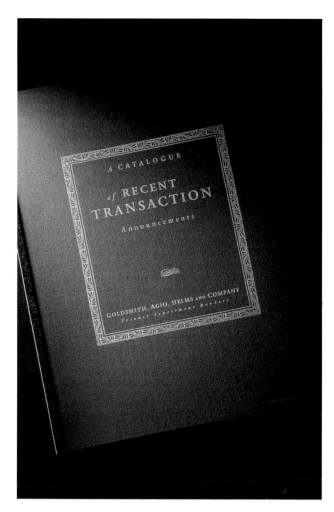

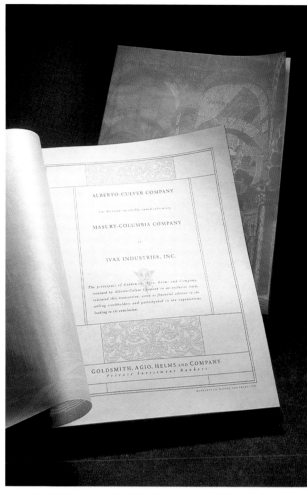

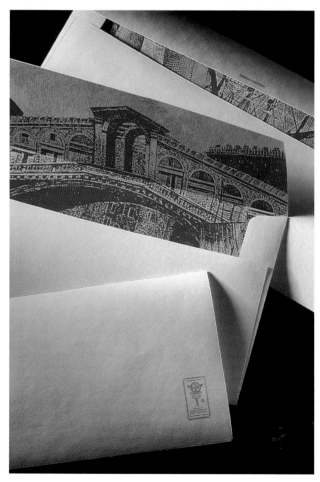

(this spread)
Hanson Associates
Arroyo Grille

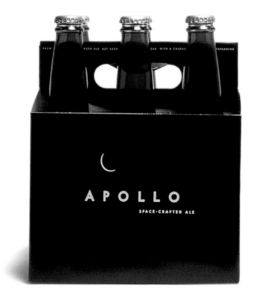

(this spread)
Cahan & Associates
Boisset USA

(this spread)
Alan Chan Design Co.
Ichizen Japanese Restaurant

(this spread)
Alan Chan Design Co.
Liverpool-Shanghai Tea Company, Ltd.

(this spread)
The Leonhardt Group
Zio Ricco

(this spread)
Hornall Anderson Design Works
Jamba Juice

(this spread)
Niemitz Design Group
Fire King Baking Co.

(this spread)
Graphics and Designing Inc.
G&D Management Inc.

(this page)
Design Partnership/Portland
Winmar Company, Inc.

(opposite)
Donovan & Green
Thomas J. Lipton Company

(this spread)
Sayles Graphic Design
801 Steak & Chop House

(this spread)
Sayles Graphic Design
Timbuktuu Coffee Bar

(this spread)
Alan Chan
Mandarin Oriental Cake Shop

(this spread)
Mires Design
Deleo Clay Tile Company

(this spread)
Mires Design
Deleo Clay Tile Company

(this spread)
Larsen Design & Interactive
Novellus Systems

(this spread)
Mires Design
Taylor Guitars

(this spread)
Beauchamp Group
Titanium Metals Corporation

(this spread)
TL Horton Design, Inc.
Rockwell/Collins Avionics

(this spread)
Trademark Design Limited
Alpha Limited

(this spread)
Mires Design
California Center for the Arts

(this spread)
Poulin + Morris
Indianapolis Museum of Art

O J I

PAPER

GALLERY

GINZA

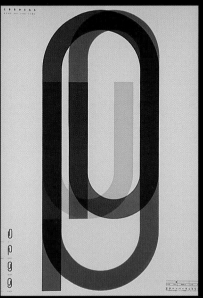

O J I PAPER GALLERY GINZA

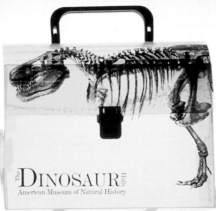

(this spread)
The ROC Company
Pitney Bowes & the National Postal Museum

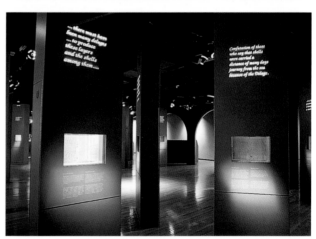

(this spread)
American Museum of Natural History
(In-house)

TAMOTSU YAGI

UNTITLED is a new fashion brand and label created by World Co., Ltd. A term commonly used to identify paintings, photographs and other works of art not titled by their authors, UNTITLED is evocative of the art world and artistic pursuits. Inspired and free-spirited, the UNTITLED collection offers the opportunity to mix and match from an eclectic palate of unique clothing and accessories. They are the raw materials from which the wearer creates her own unique composition. Hence the expression, "THE BODY IS YOUR CANVAS." UNTITLED is self expression as an art form, guided by creative intuition and imagination.

TAMOTSU YAGI

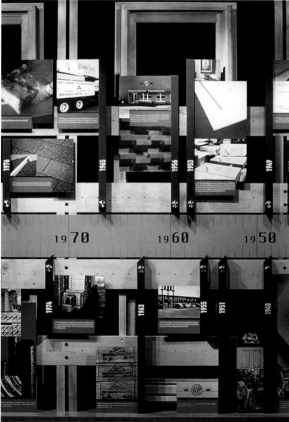

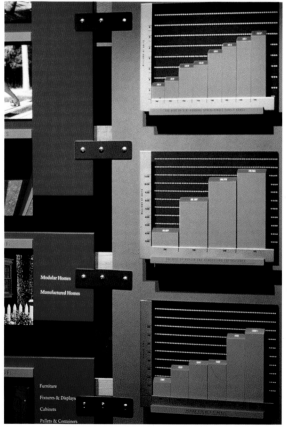

(this and following spread)
Lorenc Design
Georgia-Pacific Corporation

(this spread)
Pentagram Design Inc.
Simpson Paper Company

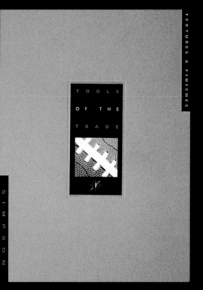

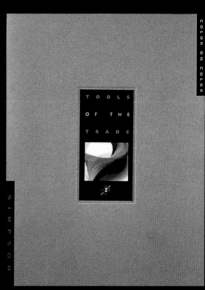

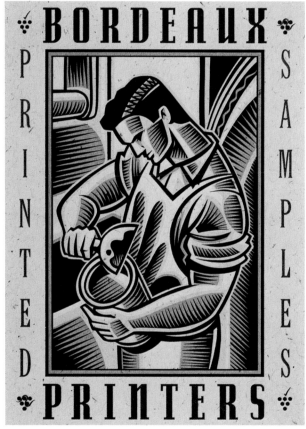

(this spread)
Mires Design
Bordeaux Printers

(this spread)
Mires Design
Bordeaux Printers

(this spread)
Gee & Chung Design
Chronicle Books

(this spread)
The Leonhardt Group
REI

(this spread)
Kiku Obata & Co.
Help-Ur-Self, Inc.

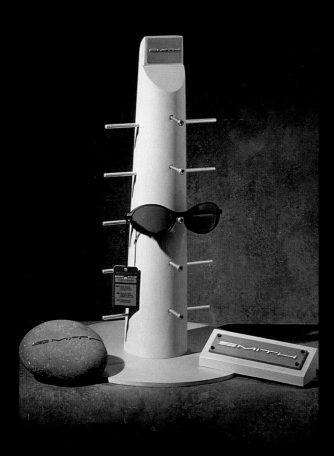

(this spread)
Hornall Anderson Design Works, Inc.
Smith Sport Optics, Inc.

(this spread)
Vaughn Wedeen Creative
Rippelstein's

(this spread)
Kiku Obata & Co.
Aaron Brothers Art & Framing

COFFEE C

Fresh Coffe

HOUSE BLEND
100% ARABICA COFFEE

HOUSE BLEND DECAF
100% ARABICA COFFEE

FLAVORED COFFEE

Half & Half Cream

PRECISION GRINDER

WASTE

(previous spread)
Antista Fairclough Design
National Convenience Stores

(this spread)
2nd Globe
(In-house)

(opposite)
Marcus Lee Design Pty., Ltd.
Paperpoint

(this page)
Marcus Lee Design Pty., Ltd.
AC TOD Quality Printing

(this spread)
Pentagram Design
Gymboree Corporation

SHAUN MCCARTHY

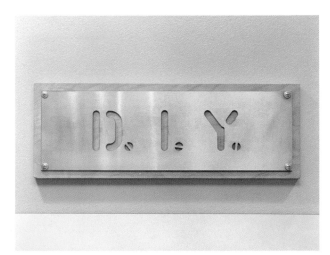

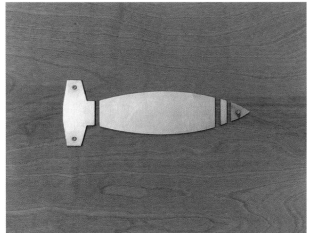

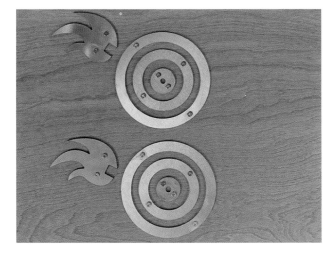

(this spread)
Brainstorm, Inc.
Shaun McCarthy Salon

(this spread)
Antista Fairclough Design
Texaco Refining & Marketing, Inc.

(this spread)
Communication Arts Inc.
The Mills Corporation

(this spread)
Communication Arts Inc.
The Mills Corporation

(this spread)
Communication Arts Inc.
Trizec Hahn

(this page)
Emery Vincent Design
Botanical Hotel

(opposite)
Emery Vincent Design
Denton Corker Marshall

(this spread)
Impact Group Inc.
Maroon Creek Club

(this spread)
K. Polesky Design
Pittsburgh Zoo

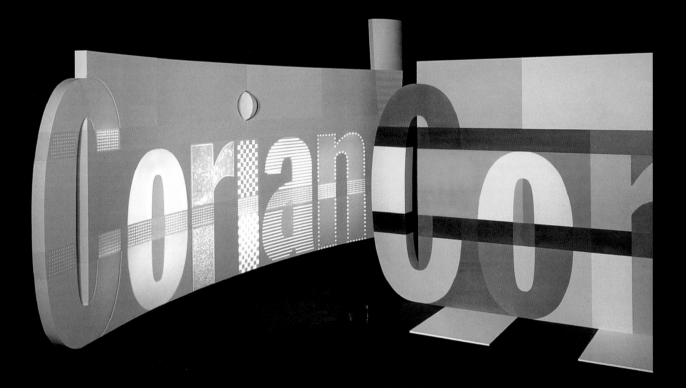

(this spread)
Pentagram Design
DuPont Company

(this spread)
Thinking Caps
City of Phoenix, AZ-Phoenix Civic Plaza

(this spread)
Thinking Caps
City of Phoenix, AZ-Phoenix Civic Plaza

(this spread)
Sommese Design
Aqua Penn Spring Water Co., Inc.

(this spread)
Sandstrom Design
Reebok

(this spread)
Nike Image Design
Nike, Inc.

SPORTS · SPORT · SPORTS

(this spread)
Pinkhaus
Lipton International Tennis Tournament

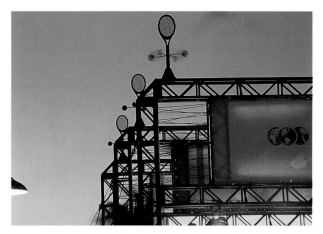

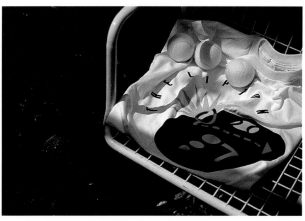

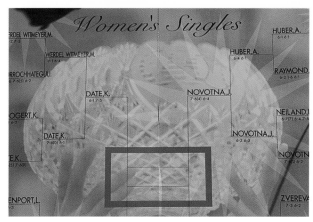

(this spread)
Küngdesign
Thai Farmers Bank

(pages 218-225)
El Estudio Shakespear
Tren de la Costa

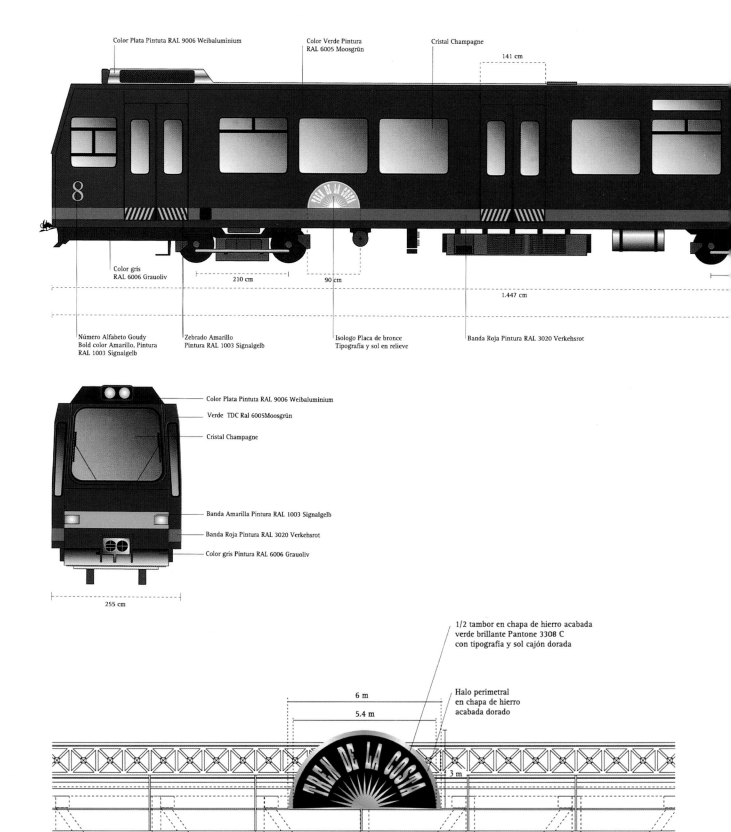

Color Plata Pintuta RAL 9006 Weibaluminium

Color Verde Pintura
RAL 6005 Moosgrün

Cristal Champagne

141 cm

Color gris
RAL 6006 Grauoliv

210 cm

90 cm

1.447 cm

Número Alfabeto Goudy
Bold color Amarillo, Pintura
RAL 1003 Signalgelb

Zebrado Amarillo
Pintura RAL 1003 Signalgelb

Isologo Placa de bronce
Tipografía y sol en relieve

Banda Roja Pintura RAL 3020 Verkehsrot

Color Plata Pintuta RAL 9006 Weibaluminium

Verde TDC Ral 6005Moosgrün

Cristal Champagne

Banda Amarilla Pintura RAL 1003 Signalgelb

Banda Roja Pintura RAL 3020 Verkehsrot

Color gris Pintura RAL 6006 Grauoliv

255 cm

1/2 tambor en chapa de hierro acabada
verde brillante Pantone 3308 C
con tipografía y sol cajón dorada

Halo perimetral
en chapa de hierro
acabada dorado

6 m

5.4 m

3 m

Cristal Champagne

Color Verde Pintura RAL 6005 Moosgrün

Color Plata Pintuta RAL 9006 Weibaluminium

14471 mm

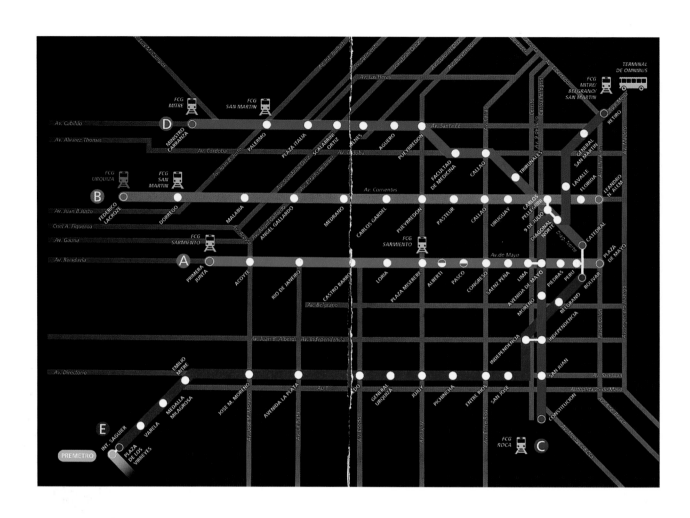

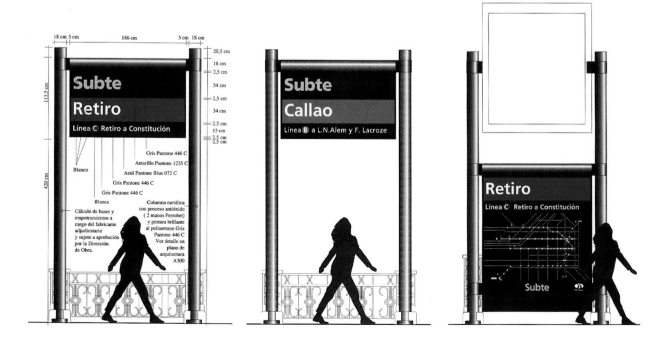

(this page)
Anita Burghard
Flughafen Münich GmbH

(opposite)
Kiku Obata & Co.
Citizens for Modern Transit

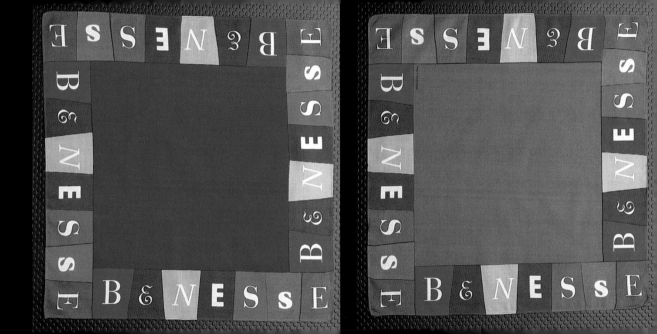

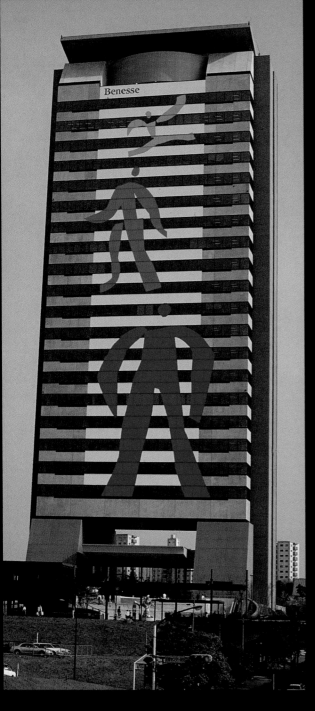
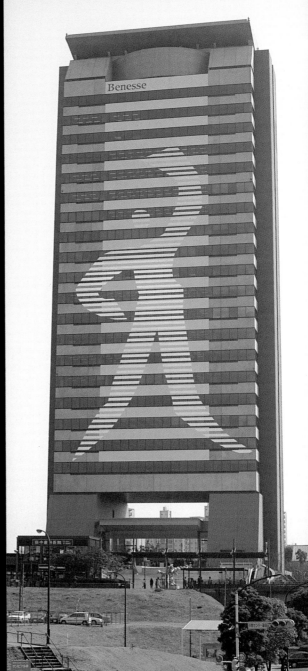

(this spread)
Shin Matsunaga
Benesse Corp.

PAGE 2 DESIGN FIRM: Mires Design CLIENT: Taylor Guitar

PAGE 4 ART DIRECTOR/DESIGNER: Earl Gee DESIGN FIRM: Gee & Chung Design PHOTOGRAPHER: Kirk Amyx FABRICATOR: Hood Exhibits CLIENT: IBM Corp.

PAGE 6 ART DIRECTOR: Michaela Bauer DESIGNER: Roland Schneider DESIGN FIRM: Bauers Büro CLIENT: Creative Modevertriebs GmbH

PAGE 28 DESIGN FIRM: Zimmerman Crowe Design CLIENT: Levi Strauss & Co.

PAGE 30 DESIGN FIRM: Mires Design CLIENT: Hot Rod Hell

PAGE 34 ART DIRECTOR/DESIGNER: Hilda Stauss Owen DESIGN FIRM: Communication Arts Company Gretchen Haien PRINTER/PAPER: (booklet covers) Hederman Brothers SIGN FABRICATOR: Ed Millet Steelworks CLIENT: Craig Singleton Hollomon Architects PRINTER: Graphic Reproductions PAPER: Strathmore Writing TYPEFACE: Trajan

PAGE 35 ART DIRECTOR: Michael Gericke DESIGNERS: Michael Gericke, Edward Chioutucto DESIGN FIRM: Pentagram Design Inc. CLIENT: American Institute of Architects ■ Identity for the American Institute of Architects, based on its acronym. ● C.I.-Design für das American Institute of Architects, basierend auf seinem Akronym. ▲ Identité visuelle de l'American Institute of Architects basée sur son acronyme.

PAGE 36, 37 ART DIRECTOR: Stan Serr DESIGNERS: Mark Jones, Dana Granoski, Dana Poon PHOTOGRAPHER: Steve Kovich DESIGN FIRM: George P. Johnson Co. MANUFACTURER: George P. Johnson Co. CLIENT: Nissan Corporation ■ To reflect brand loyalty and heritage, this identity captures the same muted color schemes commonly used in ads during the 1940s and 1950s. The campaign also features Mr. K., the charismatic Japanese man who introduced the Datsun brand to America in the 1950s. ● Um Markentreue und Tradition zum Ausdruck zu bringen, wurde hier die in den vierziger und fünfziger Jahren übliche gedämpfte Farbpalette verwendet. Die Kampagne bedient sich des charismatischen Mr. K., der in den fünfziger Jahren für die Einführung der Marke Datsun in Amerika eingesetzt wurde. ▲ Afin de refléter la longue tradition de la marque, l'agence a utilisé une palette de couleurs sourdes caractéristique des publicités des années 40 et 50. Illustration du Japonais Mr. K., personnage charismatique utilisé pour le lancement de la marque Datsun sur le marché américain.

PAGE 38, 39 ART DIRECTOR: Mark Artus DESIGNERS: Jackie Richmond, Paul Lechleiter PHOTOGRAPHER: Randy Miller DESIGN FIRM: Fitch Inc. ENVIRONMENTAL DESIGNERS: Christian Davies, Jon Baines GRAPHIC IMPLEMENTATION COORDINATOR: Christian Davies Goode CLIENT: Chrysler Corporation ■ An innovative approach to strengthening the client's brand image, the showroom does not sell cars, but only presents Chrysler's heritage and line of products. The cars are categorized around people's lifestyle needs. ● Hier ging es allen darum, Chryslers Marken-Image zu stärken. Der Ausstellungsraum dient ausschliesslich zur Präsentation der Produktpalette. Die Bedürfnisse der Käufer bestimmten das Ausstellungskonzept für die verschiedenen Modelle. ▲ Show-room présentant différents modèles Chrysler en fonction des attentes des clients et de leur style de vie. L'objectif principal consistait à renforcer l'image de marque du constructeur automobile.

PAGE 40 ART DIRECTOR/DESIGNER: José A. Serrano DESIGN FIRM: Mires Design PHOTOGRAPHER: Tracy Sabin CLIENT: Hot Rod Hell ■ The logo blends 1950s nostalgia with the modern attitude of the old-car culture. ● Das Logo reflektiert die heutige Vorliebe für Oldtimer. ▲ Le logo reflète la passion et la nostalgie des voitures anciennes.

PAGE 41 ART DIRECTOR/DESIGNER: Paul Lavoie DESIGN FIRM: TAXI Design CLIENT: Clearnet ■ This technology, exclusive in Canada, comprises a pager, two-way radio, group call and cellular telephone.

Particularly appropriate for businesses operating on the road, the identity parodies the style of a road sign. Print materials build on this metaphor and feature "Mike," a personification of the unit as "everyman" become irreverent guardian angel. ● Zu dieser Ausstattung, die nur in Kanada erhältlich ist, gehören ein Pager, Funkgeräte und ein Handy. Da dies besonders für Geschäftsleute geeignet ist, die viel unterwegs sind, wurde der Stil eines Verkehrsschildes zum prägenden Element des C.I.-Designs. Das gedruckte Material baut auf dieser Idee auf, wobei die Figur "Mike" zu einer Art Schutzengel wird. ▲ Uniquement disponible au Canada, cet équipement comprend un pager, un appareil radio et un téléphone cellulaire. Ciblant les hommes d'affaires appelés à se déplacer souvent en voiture, l'identité visuelle parodie le style d'un panneau de signalisation. Les imprimés reprennent cette image en y associant le personnage de «Mike» présenté comme un ange gardien.

PAGE 42, 43 ART DIRECTOR: Jack Anderson DESIGNERS: Jack Anderson, Mary Hermes, Mary Hutchison, David Bates, John Anicker DESIGN FIRM: Hornall Anderson Design Works PRODUCT PHOTOGRAPHER: Tom McMackin CLIENT: Nextlink Corporation TYPEFACE: Gill Sans, Eagle Book

PAGE 44, 45 ART DIRECTOR: Jack Anderson DESIGNERS: Jack Anderson, Leo Raymundo, David Bates, Suzanne Haddon, Julia LaPine, Jill Bustamante, Cliff Chung DESIGN FIRM: Hornall Anderson Design Works PHOTOGRAPHER: Tom McMackin ILLUSTRATOR: Julia LaPine CLIENT: Intermation Corporation

PAGE 46, 47 ART DIRECTOR/DESIGNER: Earl Gee DESIGN FIRM: Gee & Chung Design PHOTOGRAPHER: Kirk Amyx FABRICATOR/ACCOUNT MANAGEMENT: Hood Exhibits CLIENT: IBM Corporation TYPEFACE: Univers49, Bodoni ■ The IBM Software Station is the industry's first software "vending machine," enabling consumers to examine and purchase software directly from the kiosk. The Software Station logo symbolizes the electronic delivery of software. ● Die IBM Software Station ist die erste Software-Kiosk der Branche, die dem Konsumenten die Möglichkeit gibt, Software direkt zu testen und zu kaufen. Das Logo für die sogenannte «Vending Machine» symbolisiert die elektronische Lieferung der Software. ▲ L'IBM Software Station est le premier kiosk interactif de la branche conçu pour vendre des logiciels et permet aux consommateurs de les tester et de les acheter directement. Le logo créé pour cette «vending machine» symbolise la livraison électronique des logiciels.

PAGE 48 ART DIRECTOR: Justus Oehler DESIGNERS: Justus Oehler DESIGN ASSISTANT: Andrea Speidel DESIGN FIRM: Pentagram Design Limited CLIENT: Computer Film Company ■ The identity reflects the client's credibility and expertise as an established operator of digital film facilities. The image is one of self-assurance, but is not overstated. The design uses a thin vertical line between the "F" and the last "C" to distinguish between what the company does and who they are. ● Das Design sollte die Zuverlässigkeit und Erfahrung eines Betreibers von Filmstudios für digitale Medien reflektieren. Die dünne vertikale Linie zwischen dem F und dem letzten C soll Unternehmenszweck- und -kultur trennen. ▲ Le design reflète la fiabilité et l'expérience d'un exploitant de studios de cinémas spécialisé dans les médias numériques. La fine ligne verticale entre le F et le dernier C sert à distinguer les activités de la société de sa philosophie.

PAGE 49 ART DIRECTOR/DESIGNER: Mark Geer DESIGN FIRM: Geer Design DESIGNER: Heidi Flynn Allen CLIENT: Times 3 Productions

PAGE 50 ART DIRECTOR: Cabell Harris DESIGNER: Haley Johnson, Dan Olson DESIGN FIRM: Work, Inc. CLIENT: Work, Inc. PAPER: Scott Offset (letterhead/envelope), Springhill Bristol (rolodex)

TYPEFACES: Ludlow Condensed, Futura

PAGE 51 ART DIRECTOR: Cabell Harris DESIGNER: Tom Gibson DESIGN FIRM: Work, Inc. PHOTOGRAPHERS: Karl Steinbrenner, Jay Paul ILLUSTRATOR: Lumpy McClaning COPYWRITER: Tom Gibson CLIENT: Work, Inc. PRINTER: Worth Higgins & Associates PAPER: Cereal Box Stock ■ These baseball cards reflect the fun atmosphere of the designer's work environment. ● Diese Baseball-Karten reflektieren die Freude, die das Arbeitsumfeld des Designers prägt. ▲ Ces cartes de baseball reflètent l'atmosphère joyeuse qui caractérise l'environnement de travail du designer.

PAGE 52-55 ART DIRECTOR/DESIGNER: Pierre Mendell DESIGN FIRM: Mendell & Oberer CLIENT: Bavarian State Opera PRINTER: WKD-Offsetdruck TYPEFACES: Bodoni, Univers

PAGE 56-61 ART DIRECTOR: Paula Scher DESIGNERS: Paula Scher, Ron Louie, Ron Mazur, Jane Mella, Anke Stohlman DESIGN FIRM: Pentagram Design PHOTOGRAPHERS: Richard Avedon, Paula Court CLIENT: The Public Theater ■ The varied but cohesive graphic language reflects street typography: It's active, unconventional, and almost graffiti-like. The identity combines an "umbrella" logo with a set of "stamps" or roundels for the organization's activities. ● Die abwechslungsreiche und doch in sich geschlossene graphische Sprache ist aktiv, unkonventionell und fast Graffiti-ähnlich. Zum Erscheinungsbild gehören ein Logo und eine Art runder Stempel für die Darstellung der verschiedenen Aktivitäten des Kunden. ▲ A la fois varié et cohérent, ce langage graphique original dans le style des graffiti donne une impression de dynamisme. L'identité visuelle comprend un logo et une série de «tampons» ronds destinés à représenter les différentes activités du client.

PAGE 62 ART DIRECTOR: BJ Krivanek DESIGNER: Joel Breaux DESIGN FIRM: BJ Krivanek PHOTOGRAPHER: Jeff Kurt Petersen URBAN SOCIOLOGIST: Sonia Baez-Hernandez TEXT SOURCES: Children of Riverside FABRICATOR: Fabrication Arts CLIENT: California Tower

PAGE 63 ART DIRECTOR/DESIGNER: BJ Krivanek DESIGN FIRM: BJ Krivanek CLIENT: in-house

PAGE 64–66 bottom ART DIRECTOR/DESIGNER: BJ Krivanek DESIGNER: Joel Breaux DESIGN FIRM: BJ Krivanek CLIENT: Union Rescue Mission, Los Angeles, CA FABRICATOR: Peter Carlson Enterprises

PAGE 66 top ART DIRECTOR/DESIGNER: BJ Krivanek DESIGN ASSISTANT: David Rieger DESIGN FIRM: BJ Krivanek CLIENT: Jefferson High School, Los Angeles, CA FABRICATOR: AHR Ampersand

PAGE 67 ART DIRECTOR/DESIGNER: BJ Krivanek DESIGN FIRM: BJ Krivanek CLIENT: Union Rescue Mission, Los Angeles, CA

PAGE 68, 69 ART DIRECTOR: Kiku Obata LEAD DESIGNER: Heather Testa DESIGNERS: John Scheffel, Chris Mueller, Jane McNeely, Tim McGinty DESIGN FIRM: Kiku Obata and Company PHOTOGRAPHER: Balthazar Korab CLIENT: Grand Center ■ For a new St. Louis performing and visual arts center, the designer analyzed a section of a former downtown theater district and developed an identity that helped transform a partially deserted space into a positive and popular entertainment district. ● Hier ging es um das Erscheinungsbild für ein neues Kulturzentrum in St. Louis. Der Designer befasste sich mit dem Standort des Zentrums in einem ehemals lebendigem Theaterdistrikt. Es gelang ihm, diesem inzwischen etwas vernachlässigtem Viertel das Image eines beliebten und belebten Vergnügungsdistrikts zurückzugeben. ▲ Identité visuelle pour un nouveau centre culturel de St. Louis. Le designer s'est intéressé au quartier où se dresse ce nouveau centre, ancien haut lieu du théâtre. Il a voulu redonner vie à cet endroit délaissé aujourd'hui, en lui conférant une touche populaire et vivante à l'image du monde du spectacle.

PAGE 70, 71 ART DIRECTOR: Paula Scher PARTNER/DESIGNER: Michael

Bierut DESIGN FIRM: Pentagram Design Inc. DESIGNER: Esther Bridavsky PARTNER/ARCHITECT: James Biber ARCHITECT/ASSISTANT: Michael Zweck-Bronner DIMENSIONS: Kiosk 16' x 16'; height with needle 30' CLIENT: The Fashion Center ■ The logo for New York's Fashion Center Business Improvement District uses a whimsical button to represent the garment trade and the organization. ● Der sehr ausgefallene Knopf im Logo für ein Modezentrum in New York repräsentiert die Bekleidungsindustrie und diese Organisation. ▲ Créé pour un centre de la mode à New York, le logo illustrant un bouton fantasque symbolise l'industrie de la mode et l'organisation.

PAGE 72, 73 ART DIRECTOR: Kiku Obata LEAD DESIGNER: John Scheffel DESIGNERS: Kay Pangraze, Kathleen Robert DESIGN FIRM: Kiku Obata and Company PHOTOGRAPHER: Gary Quesada CLIENT: Great Lakes Science Center ■ The identity explores science, technology, and the environment within the context of the Great Lakes region. The logo symbolizes several different aspects of science, such as the solar system or molecules and atoms. ● Themen für das Erscheinungsbild sind Wissenschaft, Technologie und der Standort des Auftraggebers in der sogenannten Great Lakes Region. Das Logo symbolisiert verschiedene Aspekte der Wissenschaft wie das Sonnensystem oder Moleküle und Atome. ▲ La science, la technologie et la situation géographique du client dans la région des Grands Lacs constituent les thèmes de cette identité visuelle. Le logo symbolise différents aspects de la science, tels que le système solaire, les molécules ou encore les atomes.

PAGE 74 ART DIRECTOR/PRINCIPAL DESIGNER: Deborah Sussman DESIGN FIRM: Sussman/Prejza & Co., Inc. PROJECT MANAGERS: Debra Valencia, Yuki Nishinaka DESIGN TEAM: Hsin Hsein Tsai, Paula Loh, Natalie Rosbottom CLIENT: City of Santa Monica, CA ■ The city's logo provides visual continuity for the new signing program for city streets and parks. The 1996-1997 Bike Map illustrates the city's cycling routes: off-road beach paths, on-street bike lanes and routes. ● Das Logo der Stadt Santa Monica verleiht dem neuen Beschilderungsprogramm für Strassen und Parks ein einheitliches Gesicht. Die Karte 1996-97 für Fahrradfahrer zeigt die speziellen Fahrradspuren auf den Strassen sowie auch abseits gelegene Wege am Strand. ▲ Le logo confère une homogénéité visuelle au nouveau programme signalétique développé pour les rues et les parcs de Santa Monica. La carte 1996-97 présente le réseau des pistes cyclables de la ville et des chemins le long de la plage.

PAGE 75 ART DIRECTOR: Linda Kondo DESIGNERS: Robert Merk, April Skinnard DESIGN FIRM: Clifford Selbert Design Collaborative CLIENT: Salem State College FABRICATOR: Design Communications

PAGE 76, 77 ART DIRECTOR: Fabian Schmid DESIGNERS: Fabian Schmid, Andrea English DESIGN FIRM: Werkhaus Design ILLUSTRATOR: Werkhaus Design, Doug Dahler CLIENT: Snohomish County Parks Dept. PRINTER: Signtech TYPEFACE: Frutiger ■ The signage uses materials that will age over time to integrate with the natural environment. ● Für diese Beschilderung wurden Materialien ausgewählt, die mit der Zeit altern, damit sie sich ihrer natürlichen Umgebung anpassen. ▲ Signalétique créée avec des matériaux qui se patinent avec le temps afin de les intégrer à leur environnement naturel.

PAGE 78, 79 ART DIRECTOR/DESIGNER: Joe C. Nicholson DESIGN FIRM: Nicholson Design ILLUSTRATOR: Chris Paluso PHOTOGRAPHY: Eric Studer Photography CLIENT: National City, CA ■ The signage gives civic identity to a community whose main industry is automobile sales. The entire town becomes an outdoor historical car museum. ● Beschilder-ungsprogramm für eine Gemeinde, die von der Autoindustrie geprägt ist. Die ganze Stadt wird zu einem

«Freiluftmuseum der Automobilgeschichte». ▲ Programme de signalétique pour une ville dont la principale activité est l'industrie automobile. La ville entière devient un «musée en plein air de l'histoire de l'automobile».

PAGE 80 Designer: Victoria Kirk Design Firm: Desgrippes Gobé & Associates Photographer: Andrew Bordwin Design Director/ Project Manager: Mary Meuer Client: Ann Taylor Inc. ■ For a new apparel line reminiscent of an urban residential loft space, the store incorporates whitewashed brick walls, wooden trusses, skylights, and freestanding fixtures, all of which appeal to younger customers. ● Hier geht es um eine neue Bekleidungslinie, die in einem Laden mit Atelier-Charakter präsentiert wird. Die weissgetünchten, gemauerten Wände, die Balken, das Oberlicht und die frei im Raum stehenden Gestelle sprechen vor allem junge Kunden an. ▲ Nouvelle ligne de vêtements présentée dans un magasin transformé en loft. Les murs de briques badigeonnés en blanc, les poutres, l'éclairage et les présentoirs disposés librement dans l'espace s'adressent à un public cible jeune.

PAGE 81 Designers: Tom Davidson, Lora Krulak Design Firm: Desgrippes Gobé & Associates Creative Director: Peter Levine Client: Ann Taylor Inc.

PAGE 82-84 top left Art Director: Eric Thoelke Designer: Kathy Wilkinson, Reid Thompson Design Firm: Phoenix Creative Production: Gayle Van Dyke Client: Venture Design Group Typeface: Latin Bold, Schadow ■ This brand identity, for a line of jeans and casual clothing, needed to appeal to a mainstream, values-oriented audience, and improve the client's position as a retailer's premium brand. ● Dieser Markenauftritt für Jeans- und Freizeitkleidung sollte ein breites, qualitätsorientiertes Publikum ansprechen und das Image der Marke aufwerten. ▲ Identité visuelle pour une ligne de jeans et de vêtements de loisirs visant un public cible exigeant. Il s'agissait de rehausser l'image d'une grande marque.

PAGE 84 top right, bottom Art Director: Steve Morris Designer: Ed Mantels Seeker Design Firm: Venture Design Group Photographer: Ed Mantels Seeker Client: Venture Stores Printer: Shore to Shore ■ Logo for an apparel line of sturdy, sporty everyday wear for young boys and for a line of play clothes for young girls. ● Logo für strapazierfähige, sportliche Alltagskleidung für kleine Jungen und für eine Spielkleiderlinie für kleine Mädchen. ▲ Logo d'une ligne de vêtements de sport résistants pour garçons et de tenues décontractées pour filles. ■ Ivy Club is meant to conjure impressions of exemplary manner and dress with its bold, dignified color scheme and formal lines, as well as its signature line, "Since 1985." ● Hier ging es um ein gediegenes Bild des Ivy Club. ▲ Il s'agissait de transmettre une image sélect de l'Ivy Club, à l'image de ses membres.

PAGE 85 Art Director: Steve Morris Designer: Deborah Finkelstein Design Firm: Venture Design Group Client: Venture Stores Printer: Shore to Shore ■ MTO is a private-label sportswear for active, athletic boys and young men who want to stand out. The logo combines contemporary styling and handsome, confident lines. ● MTO ist eine Marke für Sportkleidung, die aktive, sportliche Jungen und junge Männer ansprechen soll, die etwas Besonderes möchten. ▲ MTO est une ligne de vêtements de sport destinée aux hommes jeunes, dynamiques et sportifs, désireux de sortir du lot. Le logo se distingue par son style moderne et l'élégance de ses lignes.

PAGE 86-89 Art Director/Designer: Stefan Sagmeister Design Firm: Sagmeister Inc. Photographer: Tom Schierlitz Backgrounds: Judith Eisler Client: Blue Printer: Vorarlberger Nachrichten Paper: Strathmore Writing Typeface: Handtype ■ The client, a fashion retailer in Austria, wanted immediate name recognition from this

identity. ● Dem Auftraggeber, einem österreichischen Modegeschäft, war die Betonung und sofortige Erkennbarkeit des Names wichtig. ▲ Le client, une boutique de mode autrichienne, désirait que le nom ressorte clairement du graphisme et soit immédiatement identifiable.

PAGE 90-91 Art Director: Roger Wong Designers: Roger Wong, Dennis Crowe Design Firm: Zimmerman Crowe Client: Levi Strauss & Co. ■ This kiosk was designed to entice 15-24-year-old male shoppers to access the Levi Strauss and Co. Web site. ● Dieser Kiosk soll junge Männer im Alter zwischen 15 und 20 Jahren dazu verleiten, die Website von Levi Strauss zu besuchen. ▲ Kiosque invitant les jeunes gens de 15 à 24 ans à visiter le site Web de Levi Strauss and Co.

PAGE 92-93 Creative Director: Brian Collins (FCB) Art Directors: Dennis Crowe, Fred Hidalgo (FCB) Designers: Dennis Crowe, Fred Hidalgo (FCB), Roger Wong, Shandele Gumucio Design Firm: Zimmerman Crowe Client: Levi Strauss & Co. Architect: Tim Gray Architecture Project Manager: Maria Mraz ■ The Levi's Men's Ultrashop was designed to appeal to the male fascination with machinery and automation. A kinetic branding wheel serves as the heart of the store. The wheel activates drive shafts that turn branding elements that move in and out of columns on the perimeter of the store. Copper, leather and steel, all original components of Levi's Jeans are incorporated into the environment. ● Der Men's Ultrashop von Levi's reflektiert die männliche Vorliebe für Maschinen und Automaten. Kernstück des Ladens ist ein kinetisches Rad, das alle möglichen Dinge in Bewegung setzt. Kupfer, Leder und Stahl, alles Bestandteile der Levi's Jeans, wurden auch für die Ausstattung des Ladens verwendet. ▲ Le concept du Levi's Men's Ultrashop reflète l'intérêt que les hommes portent à la technique et à la mécanique. Elément clé du magasin: une roue cinétique dont la rotation fait bouger divers objets. Le cuivre, le cuir et l'acier – tous les matériaux utilisés pour les jeans Levi's – sont déclinés dans la décoration d'intérieur du magasin.

PAGE 94 Art Director/Designer: José A. Serrano Design Firm: Mires Design Photographer: Dan Toner Client: Adventure 16 ■ Executed with an old engraving style, the client's new mark focuses on the beauty of the outdoors and conveys a feeling of adventure. ● Ausgeführt im Stil eines alten Stiches, konzentriert sich das neue Markenzeichen des Auftraggebers auf die Schönheit der Natur und vermittelt gleichzeitig ein Gefühl von Abenteuer. ▲ Exécuté dans le style d'une vieille estampe, le nouveau nom de marque du client reflète la beauté de la nature et véhicule en même temps un sentiment d'aventure.

PAGE 95 Art Director/Designer: José A. Serrano Design Firm: Mires Design Illustrator: Dan Toner Client: Adventure 16 ■ The goal of this project was to redesign the client's corporate identity in a way that would reflect the nature of the company. ● Die Aufgabe bestand in der Überarbeitung des visuellen Erscheinungsbildes des Auftraggebers, mit dem Ziel, das Wesen des Unternehmens besser zum Ausdruck zu bringen. ▲ La tâche de l'agence consistait à revoir l'identité visuelle du client afin de mieux faire ressortir la nature de la société. PAGE 96-97 Designer: Haley Johnson, Dan Olson Design Firm: Haley Johnson Design Co. Client: Goldsmith, Agio, Helms & Co. Printer: Diversified Graphics Paper: Starwhite Vicksburg Typeface: Adobe Garamond ■ Sophisticated, upscale identity for a young investment banking firm. ● Ein anspruchsvolles Erscheinungsbild für eine junge Investment-Firma. ▲ Identité visuelle raffinée d'une société d'investissement.

PAGE 98-99 Art Director: Gil Hanson Designer: Toby Beck Design Firm:

Hanson Associates CLIENT: Arroyo Grille ■ The identity captures the ambience of this waterfront restaurant, which serves upscale Santa Fe cuisine. ● Zentrales Thema ist die bevorzugte Lage des Restaurants am Wasser. Es gehört zur gehobenen Kategorie und bietet Spezialitäten aus Santa Fe an. ▲ Identité visuelle reflétant l'atmosphère d'un excellent restaurant de spécialités régionales situé au bord de l'eau à Santa Fe.

PAGE 100 ART DIRECTOR: Bill Cahan DESIGNER: Kevin Roberson DESIGN FIRM: Cahan & Associates ILLUSTRATOR: Kevin Roberson CLIENT: Boisset USA TYPEFACE: Futura

PAGE 101 top left & right ART DIRECTOR: Bill Cahan DESIGNER: Sharrie Brooks DESIGN FIRM: Cahan & Associates CLIENT: Boisset USA TYPEFACES: Univers, Officiana, Din Neuzeitg Grotek

PAGE 101 bottom left & bottom right ART DIRECTOR: Bill Cahan DESIGNER: Kevin Roberson DESIGN FIRM: Cahan & Associates CLIENT: Boisset Usa TYPEFACE: Hand-lettering

PAGE 102, 103 ART DIRECTOR: Alan Chan DESIGNERS: Alan Chan, Phillip Leung DESIGN FIRM: Alan Chan Design Co. ILLUSTRATOR: Hoga Lam CLIENT: Ichizen Japanese Restaurant ■ The stylized cloud logo symbolizes good fortune and happiness. ● Das Logo in Form einer stilisierten Wolke symbolisiert Glück und Zufriedenheit. ▲ Logo en forme de nuage stylisé symbolisant bonheur et joie de vivre.

PAGE 104, 105 ART DIRECTOR: Alan Chan DESIGNERS: Alan Chan, Alvin Chan, Phillip Leung DESIGN FIRM: Alan Chan Design Co. CLIENT: Liverpool-Shanghai Tea Company, Ltd. ■ The logo for this Chinese tea retail store takes the form of a traditional tea house shop's sign and is composed of the Chinese character of the shop's name. ● Das Logo für einen chinesischen Teeladen basiert auf einem traditionellen Teehaus-Ladenschild und dem chinesischen Schriftzeichen für den Namen des Ladens. ▲ Logo pour un magasin de thé chinois inspiré d'une enseigne traditionnelle.

PAGE 106, 107 ART DIRECTOR: Janet Kruse DESIGNER: Traci Daberko DESIGN FIRM: The Leonhardt Group ILLUSTRATOR: Julie Paschkis CLIENT: Zio Ricco

PAGE 108, 109 ART DIRECTOR: Jack Anderson DESIGNERS: Jack Anderson, Lisa Cerveny, Lisa Haddon DESIGN FIRM: Hornall Anderson Design Works ILLUSTRATOR: Mits Katayama PRODUCT PHOTOGRAPHER: Tom McMackin CLIENT: Jamba Juice PRINTER: Lithographix PAPER: Various TYPEFACE: Meta, Bembo

PAGE 110, 111 CREATIVE DIRECTORS: Brad Copeland, George Hirthler ART DIRECTOR: David Butler 2D DESIGNERS: David Butler, Mark Ligameri DESIGN FIRM: Copeland Hirthler Design & Communications ACCOUNT EXECUTIVE: Jean Paris PRODUCERS/ PRODUCTION MANAGERS: Laura Perlee, Donna Harris, Tof Gunderson CLIENT: Chick-Fil-A PAPER: Recycled TYPEFACE: Franklin Gothic Condensed Bold ■ This project brands a new fast-food concept by the client. ● Hier ging es um ein neues Fastfood-Konzept des Auftraggebers. ▲ Design créé pour un nouveau concept de restauration rapide.

PAGE 112, 113 DESIGN FIRM: Niemitz Design Group CLIENT: Fire King Baking Co.

PAGE 114, 115 ART DIRECTOR: Toshihiro Onimaru DESIGNER /ILLUSTRATOR: Do DESIGN FIRM: Graphics and Designing Inc. CLIENT: G&D Management Inc. ■ Identity for restaurant/cafe in Tokyo where G&D Management, a subsidiary of Graphics & Designing, is based. ● Erscheinungsbild für ein Restaurant/ Café in Tokio, das der Designfirma Graphics and Designing Inc. gehört. ▲ Identité visuelle d'un café-restaurant de Tokyo appartenant à l'agence de design G&D Management Inc.

PAGE 116 DESIGN FIRM: Design Partnership/Portland ■ Identity and architectural graphics program for a regional retail shopping mall located in Tigard, Oregon (a suburb of Portland, Oregon). ● Erschein-ungsbild, einschliesslich Gebäudegraphik, für ein Einkaufs-zentrum in einem Vorort von Portland, Oregon. ▲ Identité visuelle et programme de graphisme architectural pour un centre commercial situé à la périphérie de Portland, Oregon.

PAGE 117 CREATIVE DIRECTOR: John Drews DESIGNER: Vanessa Ryan, John Chu DESIGN FIRM: Donovan & Green CLIENT: Thomas J. Lipton Company ■ When the client decided to extend its brand into a retail format, the designer created the Lipton "Teahouse," along with the logo design, and applied the identity to uniforms, packaging, serviceware, merchandising, and signage. ● Die Aufgabe bestand in einer Erweiterung des Lipton-Markenzeichens auf den Ladenbereich. Es entstand das Lipton-Teehaus und ein Logo, das auf Personaluniformen, Verpackung, Geschirr, Merchandising-Artikeln und Beschild-erung verwendet wird. ▲ Extension de la marque Lipton à un magasin et à un logo appliqué sur les tenues du personnel, les packagings, la vaisselle, des articles de merchandising et la signalétique.

PAGE 118, 119 ART DIRECTOR/DESIGNER: John Sayles DESIGN FIRM: Sayles Graphic Design CLIENT: 801 Steak & Chop House ■ The design and graphics for this restaurant reflect the feel of a 1920s steakhouse. Graphic elements and elegant colors and materials are found on everything from the wine list and dessert menu to toothpick wrappers and matchboxes. ● Gestaltung und graphisches Material sorgen bei diesem Restaurant für die Atmosphäre eines Steakhouse aus den 20er Jahren. Die graphischen Elemente, die eleganten Farben und Materialien prägen alles, von der Wein- und Dessertkarte bis zu den Zündholzschachteln und dem Einwickelpapier für Zahnstocher. ▲ Le concept graphique de ce restaurant reflète l'atmosphère d'un steakhouse des années 20. Les éléments graphiques, les couleurs raffinées et les matériaux sont déclinés sur tous les objets, de la carte des vins et de celle des desserts aux allumettes, en passant par les papiers des cure-dents.

PAGE 120, 121 ART DIRECTOR/DESIGNER/ILLUSTRATOR: John Sayles DESIGN FIRM: Sayles Graphic Design CLIENT: Timbuktuu Coffee Bar ■ The name "Timbuktuu" evokes an imagery clearly visible in every corner of the coffee bar. The collateral material revolves around a series of graphic pictorials, featuring two tribal figures holding a coffee pot and cups over a fire, and coffee beans and spears surrounding an ancient mask. ● Timbuktuu, der Name dieser Kaffeebar, prägte die Dekoration des gesamten Lokals. Das übrige Material zeigt eine Reihe von graphischen Darstellungen, in denen zwei Eingeborene zu sehen sind, die eine Kaffeekanne und Tassen über ein Feuer halten, sowie Kaffeebohnen und Speere, die eine alte Maske einrahmen. ▲ La décoration d'intérieur s'inspire du nom du café «Timbuktuu». Les imprimés présentent une série d'images graphiques: deux aborigènes tenant une cafetière et des tasses au-dessus d'un feu ainsi que des grains de café et des lances entourant un masque.

PAGE 122, 123 CREATIVE DIRECTOR/ART DIRECTOR/DESIGNER: Alan Chan DESIGNER: Phillip Leung DESIGN FIRM: Alan Chan Design Co. CLIENT: Mandarin Oriental Cake Shop

PAGE 124 ART DIRECTOR: José A. Serrano DESIGNERS: José A. Serrano, Miguel Perez DESIGN FIRM: Mires Design ILLUSTRATOR: Nancy Stahl CLIENT: Deleo Clay Tile Company ■ Point of Purchase display used by distributors to promote a new tile. ● Ein Ladendisplay, mit dem für eine neue Kachel des Auftraggebers geworben wird. ▲ Présentoir de magasin destiné à une nouvelle ligne de carreaux du client.

PAGE 125 ART DIRECTOR/DESIGNER: José A. Serrano DESIGN FIRM: Mires Design CLIENT: Deleo Clay Tile Company ■ The best sales tool the client had was its product, so the designer developed boxes that could economically ship roofing tile samples to customers. The earthy but detailed design conveys the fine craftsmanship and natural qualities of the clay tiles inside. ● Das beste Verkaufsinstrument des Auftraggebers ist sein Produkt. Der Designer entwarf deshalb Schachteln, in denen die Dachziegelmuster an Kunden wirtschaftlich versandt werden können, und die gleichzeitig die hervorragende Qualität und natürlichen Eigenschaften der Dachziegel widerspiegeln. ▲ Le meilleur outil de vente du client étant son produit, le designer a conçu des boîtes d'échantillonnage de tuiles pouvant être envoyées au client. Le graphisme reflète l'excellente qualité et les propriétés naturelles du produit.

PAGE 126 ART DIRECTOR/DESIGNER: José A. Serrano DESIGNER: Eric Freedman DESIGN FIRM: Mires Design ILLUSTRATOR: Nancy Stahl CLIENT: Deleo Clay Tile Company ■ The graphic look reinforces the old-world craftsmanship of the product. ● Die graphische Gestaltung reflektiert die sorgfältige Herstellung des Produktes. ▲ Graphisme reflétant la qualité de fabrication du produit.

PAGE 127 top left, top right, bottom left ART DIRECTOR/DESIGNER: José A. Serrano DESIGNER: Francoise Lemieux DESIGN FIRM: Mires Design ILLUSTRATOR: Nancy Stahl CLIENT: Deleo Clay Tile Company ■ The designer created a graphic look that reinforces the old-world craftsmanship of the product. ● Die graphische Gestaltung reflektiert die sorgfältige Herstellung des Produktes. ▲ Graphisme reflétant la qualité de fabrication du produit.

PAGE 127 bottom right ART DIRECTOR/DESIGNER: José A. Serrano DESIGN FIRM: Mires Design ILLUSTRATORS: Tracy Sabin, Nancy Stahl CLIENT: Deleo Clay Tile Company ■ This packaging needed to work as a shipping box as well as a point of purchase. The designer used a kraft cardboard box to reflect the natural quality of clay tile, and created a diestrike feature of the male figure, which pops up and functions as a point of purchase. ● Die Packung musste sich sowohl für den Versand als auch für die Präsentation im Laden eignen. Der verwendete Karton reflektiert das natürliche Material der Dachziegel, während die Pop-up-Figur für Aufmerksamkeit im Laden sorgt. ▲ Ce packaging est utilisé à la fois comme un colis postal et un présentoir de magasin. Le carton en papier craft reflète les qualités naturelles du produit, tandis que le pop-up vise à retenir l'attention des clients.

PAGE 128, 129 CREATIVE DIRECTOR: Tim Larsen ART DIRECTOR: Donna Root DESIGNER: Sascha Boecker DESIGN FIRM: Larsen Design & Interactive CLIENT: Novellus Systems ■ A high-tech-looking logo was created for the client, a leading innovator and manufacturer of advanced chemical vapor deposition systems, which are used by the semiconductor industry. ● Ein Logo im Hightech-Look für einen innovativen Markführer im Bereich der Herstellung von modernen Ablagerungssystemen für chemische Dämpfe, wie sie in der Halbleiter-Industrie verwendet werden. ▲ Logo high-tech pour un des premiers fabricants de systèmes de stockage de vapeur chimique utilisés dans le secteur des semi-conducteurs.

PAGE 130, 131 bottom right ART DIRECTOR: Scott Mires DESIGNER: Scott Mires, Miguel Perez DESIGN FIRM: Mires Design PHOTOGRAPHER: Chris Wimpey CLIENT: Taylor Guitar PRINTER: Woods Lithography PAPER: Quintesence

PAGE 131 top left & right ART DIRECTOR: Scott Mires DESIGNERS: Miguel Perez DESIGN FIRM: Mires Design ILLUSTRATOR: Michael Schwab CLIENT: Taylor Guitars PRINTER: Woods Lithography PAPER: Quintesence ■ The Taylor line of apparel was inspired by the pride felt by owners of Taylor Guitars. ● Die Beliebtheit der Taylor-Gitarren führte zur Entwicklung einer Bekleidungslinie unter diesem Markenzeichen. ▲ Le succès des guitares Taylor a débouché sur une ligne de vêtements du même nom.

PAGE 131 middle left ART DIRECTOR: Scott Mires DESIGNERS: Miguel Perez, Scott Mires DESIGN FIRM: Mires Design PHOTOGRAPHER: Chris Wimpey CALLIGRAPHY: Judythe Sieck CLIENT: Taylor Guitar PRINTER: Rush Press PAPER: Confetti & Quintessence ■ To market $10,000 limited-edition guitars, the designer created a hand-sewn, limited-edition catalog. It's very tactile and simply elegant. ● Ein handgebundener Katalog mit Fadenheftung in limitierter Auflage für eine limitierte Stückzahl von Gitarren, die für $10'000 pro Stück angeboten werden. ▲ Catalogue relié à la main au moyen d'un fil et publié en série limitée pour des guitares vendues $ 10'000 pièce.

PAGE 131 middle right ART DIRECTOR: Scott Mires DESIGNERS: Miguel Perez, Scott Mires DESIGN FIRM: Mires Design CLIENT: Taylor Guitar PRINTER: Woods Lithography PAPER: Quintesence ■ This point of purchase, a classic, old-style sign, was distributed to retail stores and is vapor-filled rather than colored glass. The sign capitalizes on the "coolness" of the sign and captures the client's logo as closely as possible. ● Das für den Einzelhandel bestimmte Schild im klassischen Stil interpretiert das Logo des Gitarrenherstellers so originalgetreu wie möglich. ▲ Destinée aux magasins de détail, cette enseigne de style traditionnel s'inspire du logo du client, un fabricant de guitares.

PAGE 131 bottom left ART DIRECTOR: Scott Mires DESIGNERS: Miguel Perez, Scott Mires DESIGN FIRM: Mires Design CLIENT: Taylor Guitars PRINTER: Woods Lithography PAPER: Quintesence ■ The shape of a guitar pick is used, naturally, as a hang tag. The shape gives the tags a unique, creative look. ● Originelles Anhänge-Etikett in Form eines Plektrons für die Kleiderlinie eines Gitarrenherstellers. ▲ Etiquette originale en forme de plectre destinée à la ligne de vêtements d'un fabricant de guitares.

PAGE 132, 133 ART DIRECTOR: Errol Beauchamp DESIGNERS: Mark Adorney, Jonas Tempel, Marguerite Broyles DESIGN FIRM: Beauchamp Group PHOTOGRAPHER: Ron Pollard FABRICATOR: Heritage CLIENT: Titanium Metals Corporation ■ The exhibition incorporates titanium into the fabrication of the kiosk and wall panels. It uses the client's product, titanium, and a visual presentation of consumer and industrial titanium products. ● Titanium, das Produkt des Auftraggebers, wurde beim Bau des Ausstellungsstandes verwendet und auch in Form von Konsum- und Industrieprodukten präsentiert. ▲ Le produit du client, le titane, a été intégré dans la fabrication du stand et des panneaux muraux et présenté sous forme de produits industriels et de consommation.

PAGE 134, 135 ART DIRECTOR: Tony L. Horton DESIGN FIRM: TL Horton Design, Inc. PHOTOGRAPHER: Gary Zvonkovic/Aker Zvonkovic Photography CLIENT: Rockwell/Collins Avionics ■ In illustrating Rockwell/Collins's exhibit, the designer displayed sensitivity to the high-tech information at the exhibit's core, while keeping the display inviting, sculptural, and creative. ● Bei dieser Ausstellung ging es vor allem um Hightech-Informationen, die auf einladende, kreative Weise präsentiert werden sollten. ▲ Pour cette exposition des produits Rockwell/Collin's, il s'agissait avant tout de transmettre de façon séduisante et créative des informations complexes ayant trait au secteur high-tech.

PAGE 136, 137 ART DIRECTOR/DESIGNER: Clive Gay DESIGN FIRM: Trademark Design Limited PHOTOGRAPHER: Mike Robinson CLIENT: Alpha Limited TYPEFACE: Customized/Gill San ■ To increase brand awareness for the client, the largest manufacturer of construction products in the southern hemisphere, the designer introduced a mnemonic symbol to the logo, and identified the corporation with the color blue. ● Die Aufgabe bestand darin, der Marke des grössten Herstellers von Baumaterialien in der südlichen Hemisphäre zu mehr Aufmerksamkeit zu verhelfen. Der Designer verwendete ein mnemonisches Symbol für das Logo und identifizierte das Unternehmen mit der Farbe Blau. ▲ Pour renforcer la présence du client sur le marché, le plus grand fabricant de matériaux de construction de l'hémisphère sud, le designer a créé un symbole mnémonique.

PAGE 138 left, 139 top ART DIRECTOR: John Ball DESIGNERS: Kathy Carpentier-Moore, John Ball DESIGN FIRM: Mires Design CLIENT: California Center for the Arts PRINTER: Gordon Seven Printing TYPEFACE: Syntax ■ The designer created a strong, sophisticated, art-neutral image for this multidisciplinary art center. ● Es ging um ein starkes, anspruchsvolles Image für ein Kulturzentrum, das in Bezug auf die hier vertretenen Kunstformen neutral sein musste. ▲ L'image forte et sophistiquée créée pour ce centre culturel multidisciplinaire devait rester neutre afin de ne pas représenter un courant artistique en particulier.

PAGE 138 right ART DIRECTOR: John Ball DESIGNERS: John Ball, Miguel Perez DESIGN FIRM: Mires Design ILLUSTRATOR: (folder) Jim Kopp CLIENT: California Center for the Arts PRINTER: Rush Press ■ The designer created a strong, sophisticated, art-neutral image for this multidisciplinary art center. ● Hier ging es um ein starkes, anspruchsvolles Image für ein Kulturzentrum, das in Bezug auf die hier vertretenen Kunstformen neutral sein musste. ▲ L'image forte et sophistiquée créée pour ce centre culturel multidisciplinaire devait rester neutre afin de ne pas représenter un courant artistique en particulier.

PAGE 139 bottom ART DIRECTOR: John Ball DESIGNERS: John Ball, Gail Spitzley DESIGN FIRM: Mires Design COPYWRITER: Reece Shaw CLIENT: California Center for the Arts PRINTER: Bordeaux PAPER: Northwest Gloss, Champion Corwain, Classic Crest TYPEFACE: Custom Typography & Avenir ■ To represent an exhibition catalog of animal-inspired art, the "l"s in "wildlife" are made into eyes set on a mysterious black background. ● Katalog für eine Ausstellung von Kunst, die von Tieren inspiriert wurde. Geheimnisvolle Augen ersetzen die i-Punkte des Wortes "Wildlife". ▲ Catalogue pour une exposition d'art animalier. Des yeux mystérieux remplacent les points sur les «i» du mot «Wildlife».

PAGE 140, 141 ART DIRECTOR/DESIGNER: Richard Poulin DESIGN FIRM: Poulin + Morris FABRICATOR: Cornelius Architectural Products CLIENT: Indianapolis Museum Of Art ■ This design program included the development of all environmental graphics and wayfinding sign elements, exterior banners and site signs, stationery, public information brochures, a monthly magazine, promotional materials, and exhibition interpretive graphics for the museum's major collections. ● Zu diesem Design-Programm für das Kunstmuseum von Indianapolis gehörten die Aussenbeschilderung, einschliesslich Leitsysteme, Flaggen für draussen und Architekturgraphik sowie Informationsbroschüren für das Publikum, ein monatlich erscheinendes Magazin, Promotionsmaterial und die graphische Gestaltung für die Ausstellungen der wichtigsten Sammlungen des Museums. ▲ Programme de design pour le musée des Beaux-Arts d'Indianapolis comprenant la signalétique, des bannières, des éléments de graphisme environnemental, du papier à lettres, des brochures pour le public, un magazine mensuel et le concept graphique pour les expositions des principales collections du musée.

PAGE 142, 143 ART DIRECTOR: Akio Okumura DESIGNER: Emi Kajihara DESIGN FIRM: Packaging Create, Inc. CLIENT: Oji Paper Co., Ltd.

PAGE 144, 145 ART DIRECTOR: Paula Scher DESIGNERS: Paula Scher, Lisa Mazur, Jane Mella, Ron Louie DESIGN FIRM: Pentagram Design, Inc. CLIENT: American Museum of Natural History TYPEFACE: Devinne ■ The primary goal of the design program was to create an overall identity that would unite the broad variety of programs that had developed separately within the institution. The new logo and graphic identity coincided with the museum's 125th anniversary. ● Das Hauptanliegen war die Schaffung eines homogenen Erscheinungsbildes, das die Vielfalt der innerhalb des Museums entwickelten Programme vereinen soll. Das neue graphische Erscheinungsbild, einschliesslich des neuen Logos, war rechtzeitig zum 125. Jahrestag des Museums fertig. ▲ Objectif: créer une identité visuelle homogène établissant un lien entre les différents programmes développés individuellement au sein du musée. La nouvelle identité graphique, incluant un logo, a pu être présentée à l'occasion du 125ème anniversaire du musée.

PAGE 146, 147 ART DIRECTOR: Nancy Campbell, Mark Richardson DESIGNERS: Mark Richardson, Mark Lacko, Doug Winner, Wendy Oppel, David LaPorta, Erica Hess DESIGN FIRM: The ROC Company COPYWRITER: Nancy Campbell CLIENTS: Pitney Bowes, the National Postal Museum ■ The designer used advanced technology to show the impact of direct mail from the 19th century to the present in the United States. ● Mit Hilfe der neuen Technologie wurde die Entwicklungsgeschichte der Direct Mailings in den USA vom 19. Jahrhundert bis heute dargestellt. ▲ Le designer a utilisé des technologies avancées pour illustrer l'histoire des mailings aux Etats-Unis du 19ème siècle à nos jours.

PAGE 148, 149 DESIGNER: Willard Whitson DESIGN FIRM: American Museum of Natural History, Exhibition Department AUTHOR: Craig Morris CLIENT: American Museum of Natural History ■ This exhibit reveals the "unknown" Leonardo through a reverence for the original documents. ● In dieser Ausstellung wird dem Publikum mit Hilfe von Originaldokumenten der weniger bekannte Leonardo da Vinci vorgestellt. ▲ Cette exposition vise à mieux faire connaître Léonard de Vinci au public par le biais de documents originaux.

PAGE 150, 151 ART DIRECTOR/DESIGNER: Tamotsu Yagi DESIGN FIRM: Tamotsu Yagi CLIENT: Self-promotion/San Francisco Museum of Modern Art

PAGE 152-155 ART DIRECTOR: Jan Lorenc DESIGNERS: Jan Lorenc, Rory Myers, Gary Flesher DESIGN FIRM: Lorenc Design ILLUSTRATOR: Rion Rizzo CLIENT: Georgia-Pacific Corporation ■ This exhibit, for a wood-products company's sales center, incorporates the company's products and history into a storyline that allows visitors to touch and feel the details in the merchandise. ● Diese Ausstellung im Verkaufszentrum einer Firma der Holzindustrie erzählt die Geschichte des Unternehmens mit Hilfe seiner Produkte, wobei der Besucher sie berühren, die Details ertasten kann. ▲ Cette exposition dans le point de vente d'une société de l'industrie de bois raconte l'histoire de l'entreprise par le biais de ses produits. Les visiteurs sont invités à toucher et à sentir la qualité des matériaux.

PAGE 156, 157 ART DIRECTOR: Kit Hinrichs DESIGNERS: Belle How, Amy Chan DESIGN FIRM: Pentagram Design Co. CLIENT: Simpson Paper Co.

PAGE 158 ART DIRECTOR: José A. Serrano DESIGNERS: José A. Serrano, Miguel Perez DESIGN FIRM: Mires Design ILLUSTRATOR: Tracy Sabin CLIENT: Bordeaux Printers ■ The client's name, Bordeaux Printers, allowed the designer to link visually the fine art of wine-making with the fine art of printing, suggesting the old-world craftsmanship common to both. ● Der Name des Auftaggebers, Bordeaux

Printing, erlaubte den Vergleich der Kunst des Kelterns mit der Kunst des Druckens. ▲ Le nom du client, Bordeaux Printing, a incité le designer à comparer l'art de la vinification à celui de l'impression.

PAGE 159 DESIGNERS: José Serrano, Miguel Perez DESIGN FIRM: Mires Design ILLUSTRATOR: Tracy Sabin CLIENT: Bordeaux Printers ■ To communicate the image of high-end printing, the client's sales representatives and production people signed these labels and tags to show that the printed samples had been carefully inspected. ● Im Sinne des hohen Qualitätsanspruchs der Druckerei wurden diese Etiketten und Anhänger von Vertretern und Produktionsleuten signiert, quasi als Zeichen einer sorgfältigen Qualitätskontrolle der Druckerzeugnisse. ▲ Pour refléter les critères de qualité de cette imprimerie, les représentants et les gens de la production ont apposé leur signature sur ces étiquettes pour confirmer que les épreuves d'impression avaient été contrôlées avec minutie.

PAGE 160 top ART DIRECTOR: José A. Serrano DESIGNERS: José A. Serrano, Miguel Perez DESIGN FIRM: Mires Design ILLUSTRATORS: Gerry Bustamante, Margaret Cashara, Roxana Villa, Normand Cousineau, Terry Widener COPYWRITER: Kelly Smothermon CLIENT: Bordeaux Printers ■ This corporate identity's emphasis on quality and craftsmanship is communicated in these mailers. ● Qualität und handwerkliches Können sind die Themen dieses Werbeaussands für eine Druckerei. ▲ Publipostage pour une imprimerie mettant en exergue la qualité et le savoir-faire du client.

PAGE 160 bottom DESIGNER: José Serrano, Miguel Perez DESIGN FIRM: Mires Design ILLUSTRATOR: Tracy Sabin CLIENT: Bordeaux Printers ■ These labels and tags were used as part of a quality-assurance program. ● Die Etiketten und Anhänger gehören zu einem Programm, dessen Thema die hohe Qualität der Druckerzeugnisse des Auftraggebers ist. ▲ Etiquettes appartenant à un programme mettant l'accent sur la qualité des épreuves d'impression du client.

PAGE 161 ART DIRECTOR: José A. Serrano DESIGNERS: José A. Serrano, Miguel Perez DESIGN FIRM: Mires Design ILLUSTRATOR: Tracy Sabin CLIENT/PRINTER: Bordeaux Printers ■ This identity linked the fine art of wine-making to that of printing. ● Das zentrale Thema ist hier der Vergleich der Kunst des Kelterns mit der Kunst des Druckens. ▲ La comparaison entre l'art de la vinification et celui de l'impression représente ici le thème principal.

PAGE 162-165 ART DIRECTOR/DESIGNER: Earl Gee DESIGN FIRM: Gee & Chung Design PHOTOGRAPHER: Alan Shortall FABRICATOR: Barr Exhibits CLIENT: Chronicle Books TYPEFACE: Copperplate 33BC ■ The client's gift division sought a comfortable environment to display its greeting cards, calendars, and appointment books. The modular design is both highly functional and projects an innovative, friendly, and intelligent image for the publisher. They also needed an exhibit capable of displaying a large number of books in many ways for the ABA Show. ● Chronicle Books' Abteilung für Geschenkartikel benötigte geeignete Gestelle für die Präsentation ihrer Grusskarten, Kalender und Agendas. Das aus variablen Versatzstücken bestehende Design ist ausgesprochen praktisch und wirkt freundlich und innovativ. Zusätzlich wurden Gestelle für die Präsentation einer grossen Anzahl von Büchern an einer Messe benötigt. ▲ Outre des étagères destinées à exposer un grand nombre de livres à l'occasion du salon ABA, le rayon d'articles cadeau du magasin Chronicle Books avait besoin de présentoirs pour ses cartes de vœux, calendriers et agendas. Modulaire et pratique, le design donne une image à la fois novatrice et

conviviale de cette maison d'édition.

PAGE 166, 167 ART DIRECTOR: Mark Popich DESIGNERS: Mark Popich, R. Brengman, J.M. Harper (Corbin Design) DESIGN FIRM: The Leonhardt Group CLIENT: REI ■ The client, a provider of quality outdoor gear and equipment, has a corporate identity that reflects its environmentalist values and culture. ● Das Erscheinungsbild von REI, einem Hersteller von Freizeitkleidung und Ausstattungen, reflektiert Umweltfreundlichkeit und Kultur der Firma. ▲ L'identité visuelle de REI, un fabricant d'équipements et de vêtements de loisirs, reflète la culture de la société et son souci pour le respect de l'environnement.

PAGE 168, 169 ART DIRECTOR: Kiku Obata DESIGNERS: Kiku Obata, Idie McGinty, Tim McGinty, Jim Keane (AIA), Jane McNeely, Sylvia Teng, Kim Tunze DESIGN FIRM: Kiku Obata & Company PHOTOGRAPHER: Ed Massery CLIENT: Help-Ur-Self, Inc. ■ For a prototype candy store, the designer created three animated characters that serve as the company's "founders." The overall concept, name, identity, store design, visual merchandising, and graphics are whimsical, and have captured the imagination of shoppers. ● Für den Prototyp eines Bonbon-Ladens dachte sich der Designer drei Zeichentrick-Figuren aus, die als «Gründer» der Firma vorgestellt werden. Das gesamte Konzept, der Name, der Auftritt, die Ladengestaltung, die Displays und die graphischen Elemente sind ein bisschen verrückt und ausgefallen. ▲ Pour le prototype d'une confiserie, le designer a créé trois personnages de dessins animés présentés comme les «fondateurs» de la société. L'ensemble du concept, le nom, l'identité, le design du magasin, les présentoirs et les éléments graphiques se distinguent par leur côté loufoque destiné à retenir l'attention des clients.

PAGE 170, 171 ART DIRECTOR: Jack Anderson PRODUCT DESIGNERS: Jack Anderson, Cliff Chung, David Bates DESIGN FIRM: Hornall Anderson Design Works, Inc. CLIENT: Smith Sport Optics, Inc. ■ This trade show exhibit helped launch a new division that sells sunglasses. It also reinforces the client's environmentally conscious image by using recyclable materials. ● Diese Ausstattung eines Messestandes diente der Lancierung von Sonnenbrillen, einer neuen Produktlinie des Auftraggebers. Durch den Einsatz wiederverwendbarer Materialien wird die umweltfreundliche Einstellung der Firma betont. ▲ Conçu pour un stand d'un salon d'exposition, ce présentoir a servi à lancer une nouvelle ligne de lunettes de soleil sur le marché. L'utilisation de matériaux recyclables témoigne de l'intérêt du client pour les aspects environnementaux.

PAGE 172, 173 ART DIRECTOR/DESIGNER: Rick Vaughn DESIGN FIRM: Vaughn Wedeen Creative COPYWRITER: David Moreno CLIENT: Rippelstein's PRINTER: Academy Printers PAPER: Confetti, Loe, Kraft TYPEFACE: Futura, Univers, Limoscript ■ A men's accessories boutique inspired this identity program, which indluded signage, stationery, in-store collateral, packaging, advertising, and direct mail. ● Das C.I.-Programm für eine Herren-Boutique mit Accessoires umfasst die Beschilderung, das Geschäfts-papier, das gesamte gedruckte Material für den Laden, Verpackungen, Anzeigen und Direktwerbung. ▲ Inspiré d'une boutique d'accessoires pour hommes, ce programme d'identité visuelle comprend des éléments de signalétique, du papier à lettres, des imprimés pour le magasin, des packagings, des publicités et des mailings.

PAGE 174, 175 ART DIRECTOR: Kiku Obata DESIGNERS: Kiku Obata, Kevin Flynn (AIA), Laura McCanna, Jeff Rifkin, Joe Floresca, David Hercules DESIGN FIRM: Kiku Obata & Company PHOTOGRAPHER: Gary Quesada CLIENT: Aaron Brothers Art & Framing ■ For two prototype custom-framing and art supply stores, the designer created an environment that inspires creativity. Each department is defined by feature walls with specialty fixtures, lighting, signage, and a suspended-ceiling element. ● Für zwei Prototyp-Läden, in denen handgemachte Rahmen und Künstlerbedarf angeboten werden, schuf der Designer ein kreatives Ambiente. Jede Abteilung wird durch charakteristische Wände mit spezieller Ausstattung, Beleuchtung, Beschilderung und einem von der Decke hängenden Element gekennzeichnet. inspiré d'une boutique d'accessoires pour hommes. ▲ Le design confère une touche créative à ces deux prototypes destinés à des magasins proposant des cadres faits à la main et des fournitures d'art. Chaque rayon présente des décorations murales spécifiques, un élément suspendu au plafond, un éclairage et une signalétique distincts.

PAGE 176, 177 ART DIRECTORS/DESIGNERS: Tom Antista, Thomas Fairclough DESIGN FIRM: Antista Fairclough Design CLIENT: National Convenience Stores ■ The client is a regional petroleum convenience-store operator. To create a friendly retail environment, the designer used illustrations and photography to create taste appeal, and to ensure and support the credibility of the offerings. ● Der Auftraggeber betreibt lokale Tankstellen-Shops. Um eine freundliche Ladenatmosphäre zu schaffen, setzte der Designer Photos und Illustrationen ein, die auch die Qualität des Angebots reflektieren. ▲ Le client exploite des stations service régionales. Afin de créer une atmosphère conviviale, le designer a utilisé des photographies et des illustrations qui reflètent la qualité de l'offre.

PAGE 178, 179 CREATIVE DIRECTORS: David Young, Jeff Laramore ART DIRECTORS: Chris Beatty, Jeff Laramore, Mark Bradley, Matt Lockett DESIGN FIRM: 2nd Globe SCULPTOR: David Kirby Bellamy COPYWRITER: David Hoppe CLIENT: 2nd Globe

PAGE 180, 181 ART DIRECTOR: Kiku Obata DESIGNERS: Kiku Obata, Idie McGinty, Tim McGinty, Jim Keane (AIA), Theresa Henriken, Jane McNeely, Pam Bliss, Lisa Bollman DESIGN FIRM: Kiku Obata & Company PHOTOGRAPHER: Cheryl Ungar CLIENT: B. Dalton ■ To create a new prototype for this nationally leading mall book retailer, the design firm developed an overall concept, a new name, identity materials, store design, visual merchandising, signage, and marketing concepts. ● Die Aufgabe bestand in der Schaffung eines neuen Prototyp-Buchladens für eine grosse Kette. Die Designfirma entwickelte ein Gesamtkonzept, einen neuen Namen, das graphische Erscheinungsbild, die Ladengestaltung, Verkaufshilfen, Schilder und Marketing-konzepte. ▲ Création d'un prototype pour une grande chaîne de libraires. L'agence de design a développé un concept global qui comprend un nouveau nom, l'identité visuelle, le design des magasins, les supports de vente, la signalétique et les concepts marketing.

PAGE 182 ART DIRECTOR: Marcus Lee DESIGNER: Michelle Mackintosh DESIGN FIRM: Marcus Lee Design Pty. Ltd. CLIENT: Paperpoint

PAGE 183 ART DIRECTOR: Marcus Lee DESIGNER: George Margaritis DESIGN FIRM: Marcus Lee Design Pty. Ltd. CLIENT: Ac Tod Quality Printing

PAGE 184, 185 ART DIRECTOR: Kit Hinrichs DESIGNER: Jackie Foshaug DESIGN FIRM: Pentagram Design Inc. CLIENT: Gymboree Corporation ■ The identity for this growing children's retail store uses a universal image of play. ● Spiel ist das Thema für das Erscheinungsbild dieses Kinderladens. ▲ L'identité visuelle de ce magasin pour enfants joue la carte du ludisme.

PAGE 186, 187 CREATIVE DIRECTOR: Chuck Johnson ART DIRECTOR: Jeff Dey DESIGNERS: Jeff Dey, Chuck Johnson, Wayne Geyer DESIGN FIRM: Brainstorm, Inc. PHOTOGRAPHER: Tim Boole THREE-DIMENSIONAL

FABRICATION/DESIGN: Mecca CLIENT: Shaun McCarthy Salon ■ Identity program for an upscale hair salon known for expert hair coloring. ● Erscheinungsbild für einen teuren Coiffeur-Salon, dessen Spezialität die Haar-Colorierung bzw. das Färben ist. ▲ Identité visuelle pour un salon de coiffure chic spécialisé dans les teintures et les colorations.

PAGE 188, 189 CREATIVE DIRECTORS/DESIGNERS: Tom Antista, Thomas Fairclough DESIGN FIRM: Antista Fairclough CLIENT: Texaco Refining & Marketing, Inc. ■ The worldwide Texaco image encompasses new ground-up sites and existing retor-fit stations. The identity offers lighter, brighter colors, softer curves, and state-of-the-art materials and components. ● Das weltweit verwendete C.I.-Design von Texaco wurde für bestehende wie auch für neue Stationen entwickelt. Neu sind die helleren, leuchtenderen Farben, sanftere Formen und moderne Materialien und Einzelteile. ▲ L'identité visuelle de Texaco présente dans les stations service du monde entier a fait l'objet d'un toilettage: couleurs plus vives et lumineuses, formes plus douces, matériaux et composants plus modernes.

PAGE 190-193 ART DIRECTOR: Henry Beer DESIGNERS: Bryan Gough, Taku Shimizu, Kelan Smith, Lydia Young, Karl Hirschmann, Dave Dute, Jr. DESIGN FIRM: Communication Arts Inc. PHOTOGRAPHER: Larry Falke PROJECT MANAGER: John Ward JOB CAPTAIN: John Mack CLIENT: The Mills Corporation ■ For the world's largest outlet mall, the overall project design, interior architecture, thematic development, signage, and graphics revolve around a "Main Street." Courtyards are filled with natural light, plant life, and water for an "outdoor" experience. ● Für das grösste Einkaufszentrum der Welt wurde das gesamte C.I. Programm, einschliesslich Innenarchitektur, Beschilderung und Graphik um das Thema «Hauptstrasse» herum aufgebaut. Innenhöfe wurden mit natürlichem Licht, Pflanzen und Wasser ausgestattet, um freie Natur zu suggerieren. ▲ Conçu pour le plus grand centre commercial du monde, ce programme d'identité visuelle – architecture d'intérieur, signalétique et graphisme inclus – s'inspire du thème «Main Street». La lumière du jour, les plantes et l'eau, éléments caractéristiques des cours intérieurs, créent un environnement naturel.

PAGE 194, 195 ART DIRECTOR: Henry Beer DESIGNERS: Mike Doyle, Leonard Thomas, Kelan Smith, Jim Babinchak DESIGN FIRM: Communication Arts Inc. PHOTOGRAPHER: Aaron Hoffman CLIENT: Trizec Hahn ■ The common space interiors, signing, and graphics of this regional shopping center are reminiscent of a Colorado mountain lodge. The natural stone waterfall, stone fireplaces, wood ceilings, and craftsman-style furnishings create an atmosphere of hospitality and warmth. ● Die Innenausstattung, Beschilderung und das graphische Material für dieses Shopping Center erinnern an eine Colorado-Berghütte. Der Naturstein-Wasserfall, die gemauerten Feuerstellen, Holzdecken und schlichten Möbel schaffen eine gastfreundliche, warme Atmosphäre. ▲ L'architecture d'intérieur, la signalétique et les éléments graphiques de ce centre commercial régional rappellent un refuge de montagne du Colorado. La chute d'eau en pierre naturelle, les foyers, les plafonds en bois et la simplicité des meubles créent une atmosphère chaleureuse et conviviale.

PAGE 196 DESIGN FIRM: Emery Vincent Design CLIENT: Botanical Hotel

PAGE 197 ART DIRECTOR: Garry Emery DESIGN FIRM: Emery Vincent Design CLIENT: Denton Corker Marshall ■ The signage, produced on large, oblique blades, became the entry markers to the exhibition spaces. ● Die auf grossen, schrägen Tafeln angebrachten

Schilder dienten zur Kennzeichnung von Messeständen. ▲ Les éléments de signalétique placés sur de grands panneaux obliques ont servi à identifier les stands d'un salon d'exposition. PAGE 198, 199 ART DIRECTORS: Scott Paramski, Sean Patrick DESIGNER: Scott Paramski DESIGN FIRM: Impact Group Inc. CLIENT: Maroon Creek Club ■ This signage system is designed to blend in with the natural environment. ● Ein Beschilderungssystem, das sich der Natur anpasst. ▲ Système de signalétique s'intégrant à l'environnement naturel.

PAGE 200, 201 CREATIVE DIRECTOR & SIGNAGE PHOTOGRAPHY: Paul Selvaggio, Pittsburgh Zoo DESIGNER: Karen Polesky DESIGN FIRM: K. Polesky Design ILLUSTRATOR: Dave Klug PHOTOGRAPHERS: Flip Nicklin (Minden Pictures), Tom Leeson, Pat Leeson, Tom Pawlesh, Gerry Ellis Nature Photography, Mitch Reardon CLIENT: Pittsburgh Zoo PRINTER: Graphitek of Vermont PAPER: 3M Scotchprint TYPEFACE: Gill Sans

PAGE 202, 203 ARCHITECT/PARTNER: James Biber DESIGN FIRM: Pentagram Design Inc. ARCHITECT/ASSOCIATE: Michael Zweck-Bronner CLIENT: DuPont Company ■ Corian is a synthetic well known to interior designers as a material for kitchen and bath countertops. This exhibit challenges that preconception with sculptural sign-walls, reproduced furniture, surface manipulations and a new color palette. ● Corian ist Innenarchitekten vor allem als Kunststoffmaterial für Oberflächen in Küche und Bad ein Begriff. Hier werden mit Hilfe einer neue Farbpalette, speziell behandelter Oberflächen und Anwendungsbeispielen die weitaus vielseitigeren Nutzungsmöglichkeiten demonstriert. ▲ Le corian, un revêtement synthétique, est principalement utilisé par les architectes d'intérieur pour les cuisines et salles de bains. Les différentes applications de ce matériau sont pésentées ici par le biais d'une nouvelle palette de coloris et des surfaces traitées selon des procédés spéciaux.

PAGE 204, 205 ART DIRECTOR/DESIGNER: Ann Morton DESIGN FIRM: Thinking Caps PHOTOGRAPHER: Bill Timmerman FABRICATOR: Smithcraft CLIENT: City of Phoenix-Phoenix Civic Plaza ■ This six-block urban facility's identity includes a way-finding system. ● Zu diesem Erscheinungsbild eines städtischen Gebäudekomplexes gehört ein Leitsystem. ▲ Destinée à un complexe immobilier urbain, cette identité visuelle comprend également une signalétique pour les piétons.

PAGE 206, 207 ART DIRECTORS: Ann Morton, Julie Henson DESIGNER: Ann Morton DESIGN FIRM: Thinking Caps PHOTOGRAPHER: Bill Timmerman ILLUSTRATORS: Ann Morton, Julie Henson FABRICATOR: Smithcraft CLIENT: City of Phoenix ■ Using historical elements within the theater, the designer created a contemporary signage system for wayfinding and room identification. ● Mit Hilfe von historischen Elementen des Theaters entwickelte der Designer ein modernes Beschilderungsprogramm, das für das Leitsystem und die Kennzeichnung von Räumen angewendet wurde. ▲ A l'aide d'éléments historiques inhérents au monde du théâtre, le designer a développé un programme de signalétique moderne qui sert à identifier les différentes pièces et à retrouver son chemin.

PAGE 208, 209 ART DIRECTORS: Kristin Breslin Sommese, Lanny Sommese DESIGNER: Amy Zuckerman DESIGN FIRM: Sommese Design PHOTOGRAPHER: Paul Hazi CLIENT: Aqua Penn Spring Water Co., Inc. PRINTER: Commercial Printing PAPER: Champion Kromekote Centura Consolidated TYPEFACE: Insignia, Industria

PAGE 210, 211 ART DIRECTOR: Sally Morrow DESIGNERS: Sally Morrow, Donjiro Ban DESIGN FIRM: Sandstrom Design PRODUCER: Brad Berman COPYWRITER: Leslee Dillon CLIENT: Reebok ■ The

graphic design, signage, and applications feature Reebok's corps of international athletes under the "Planet Reebok" theme. ● "Planet Reebok" mit der Reebok-Gruppe internationaler Athleten war das zentrale Thema für das C.I.-Programm. ▲ Programme d'identité visuelle présentant des athlètes internationaux sous le thème de la «Planet Reebok».

PAGE 212, 213 CREATIVE DIRECTOR: John Hoke DESIGN FIRM: Nike Image Design PHOTOGRAPHER: Timothy Hursley DESIGN TEAM: Mike Tiedy, John Trotter, Toki Wolf, Derek Welch, Mike Ely, Stanley Hainsworth CLIENT: Nike, Inc.

PAGE 214, 215 ART DIRECTORS/DESIGNERS: Joel Fuller, John Norman, Mark Cantor, Todd Houser DESIGN FIRM: Pinkhaus CLIENT: Lipton International Tennis Tournament PRINTER: Bellak Color

PAGE 216, 217 ART DIRECTOR: Richard Küng DESIGNER: Vicki Küng DESIGN FIRM: Küngdesign PHOTOGRAPHER/ILLUSTRATOR: Doug Adesko CLIENT: Thai Farmers Bank ■ The client sponsors two professional soccer teams in Thailand. In creating players' uniforms, the designer worked closely with the manufacturer to ensure accuracy in the translation from design to printed fabric. ● Trikots für zwei thailändische Fussballmannschaften, die von der Thai Farmers Bank gesponsert werden. Sie wurden in enger Zusammenbeit zwischen Designfirma und Hersteller produziert. ▲ Maillots créés pour deux équipes de football thaïlandaises sponsorisées par la Thai Farmers Bank. Le designer a travaillé en étroite collaboration avec le fabricant pour garantir une impression fidèle de première qualité.

PAGE 218-225 ART DIRECTORS: Ronald Shakespear, Raúl Shakespear DESIGNERS: Paula Cullaré, Juan Hitters, Fernanda Algorta, Fernanda Fridman, Sushi Prieto, Mariano Covini DESIGN FIRM: El Estudio Shakespear PROJECT DIRECTOR: Lorenzo Shakespear PROJECT CHIEFS: Lorenzo Shakespear, Christian Di Bucci

PAGE 226 ART DIRECTOR/DESIGNER: Anita Burgard PHOTOGRAPHER: Hans G. Deumling PUBLISHER: Leo Verlag CLIENT: Flughafen München ■ Consisting of a "welcome" brochure and a box containing three volumes of a book, this work was published for the opening of a new Munich airport. The purpose was to present this new building complex to the public, by showing the processes of the planning, realization, and operation of the airport, through concepts and designs based on visual qualities of the site's architecture and landscape.

PAGE 227 ART DIRECTOR: Kiku Obata DESIGNERS: Kiku Obata, Pam Bliss, Pam Knopf, Rich Nelson, John Scheffel DESIGN FIRM: Kiku Obata & Company PHOTOGRAPHY: Cheryl Ungar CLIENT: Citizens for Modern Transit ■ The Metrolink Wall of Fame was designed to recognize individual and corporate funding for a new light-rail system in St. Louis. Personalized porcelain enamel tokens were made and installed on the stainless steel wall for each contributor. ● Die "Metrolink Wall of Fame" ist den privaten und institutionellen Sponsoren eines neuen Bahnsystems in St. Louis gewidmet. Für jeden einzelnen Sponsor wurden auf der Stahltafel individuelle Porzellan-Marken angebracht. ▲ Le «Metrolink Wall of Fame» est dédié aux sponsors privés et institutionnels d'un nouveau système ferroviaire à St. Louis. La paroi en acier inoxydable présente pour chaque sponsor une marque en porcelaine.

PAGE 228-231 ART DIRECTOR/DESIGNER: Shin Matsunaga CLIENT: Benesse Corp.

PAGE 232 ART DIRECTOR/DESIGNER: Scott Paramski ART DIRECTOR: Sean Patrick DESIGN FIRM: Impact Group Inc. CLIENT: Maroon Creek Club ■ This signage system blends in with the natural environment.

IndicesVerzeichnisseIndex

Order Graphis on the Web from anywhere in the world: www.graphis.com

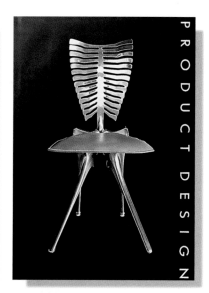

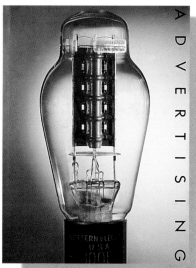

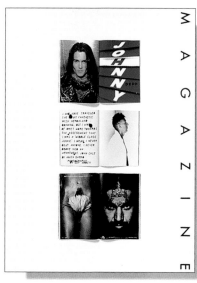

All Graphis subscribers are eligible for a 40% discount on all Graphis titles. Your Graphis subscription pays for itself if you buy only three titles per year!

Magazine

☐ One year
  (6 issues)
  USA   US$ 89.00
  Canada   US$ 99.00
  International   US$125.00

☐ Two year
  (12 issues)
  USA   US$ 159.00
  Canada   US$ 179.00
  International   US$ 235.00

☐ One year student
  subscription for students
  with copy of valid student ID
  and payment with order
  (6 issues)
  USA   US$ 59.00

Service begins with issue
that is current when ordering
is processed.

☐ Airmail surcharge
  (6 issues)
  USA   US$ 59.00
  Canada   US$ 59.00
  International   US$ 59.00

☐ Registered mail surcharge
  (6 issues)
  USA   N/A
  Canada   N/A
  International   US$ 15.00

Books

☐ Apple Design: (2nd printing)	US$ 44.95
The Work of the AppleIndustrial Design Group	
☐ Black & White Blues	
(HC) US$ 69.95 or (PB) US$ 45.95	
☐ Advertising 98	US$ 69.95
☐ Annual Reports 5	US$ 69.95
☐ Book Design	US$ 75.95
☐ Brochures 2	US$ 75.00
☐ Corporate Identity 2	US$ 75.95
☐ Design 98	US$ 69.95
☐ Ephemera	US$ 75.95
☐ Fine Art Photography 2	US$ 85.00
☐ Letterhead 3	US$ 75.00
☐ Logo 3	US$ 49.95
☐ Music Cds	US$ 75.95
☐ Nudes	US$ 39.95
☐ Packaging 7	US$ 75.00

☐ Photo 97	US$ 69.95
☐ Poster 97	US$ 69.95
☐ Product Design	US$ 69.95
☐ Student Design 97	US$ 44.95
☐ T-Shirt Design	US$ 49.95
☐ Typography 1	US$ 69.95
☐ Type Specimens	US$ 49.95
☐ Paper Specifier System GPS	US$ 395.00
(Add $30 shipping/handling for GPS)	
☐ The Human Condition:	US$ 49.95
Photojournalism 97	
☐ Passion & Line:	US$ 50.00
Photographs of Dancers by Howard Schatz	
☐ Shoreline:	US$ 85.95
The Camera at the Water's Edge	
☐ 100 Yrs. World Trademarks:	US$ 250.00
(2 volume set)	

Order Form

☐ Please bill me
☐ Check enclosed

☐ Use credit cards
  (debited in US$)

☐ Master Card
☐ American Express

☐ Visa

Card No. _____   Exp. Date _____

Cardholder Name _____   Signature _____

Name _____   Company _____

Address _____

City / State / Province _____   Zip Code _____

Country _____   Telephone _____

Fax _____   E-Mail _____

Copy or send this order form and make check payable to : Graphis Inc., 141 Lexington Ave, New York, NY 10016-8193, USA
Order Graphis on the Web from anywhere in the world: www.graphis.com